The Sunday Readings

*Commentaries on the Sunday Liturgies for the
Three Cycles, plus Holy Days and the
Supplanting Feasts*

by ALBERT J. NEVINS, M.M.

Our Sunday Visitor, Inc.
Huntington, Indiana 46750

Nihil Obstat:
Rev. Harold Bumpus, Th.D.
Censor Deputatis

Imprimatur:
✠Most Rev. W. Thomas Larkin, D.D.
Bishop of St. Petersburg
May 3, 1984

The Nihil Obstat and Imprimatur are official declarations that a book or pamphlet is free of doctrinal or moral error. No implication is contained therein that those who have granted the Nihil Obstat or Imprimatur agree with the contents, opinions or statements expressed.

Cover design by James E. McIlrath

LIBRARY OF CONGRESS CATALOG CARD NO.: 84-60748
INTERNATIONAL STANDARD BOOK NO.: 0-87973-734-4

Published, printed and bound in the U.S.A. by:
Our Sunday Visitor, Inc.
200 Noll Plaza
Huntington, Indiana 46750

734

The Sunday Readings

Commentaries on the Sunday Liturgies for the Three Cycles, plus Holy Days and the Supplanting Feasts

Contents

Introduction

This book is intended to be used in preparing for the Sunday liturgy. It is meant to be used in connection with a Bible, missal or missalette. It gives liturgical thoughts and explanations for all the readings of the three annual cycles for each Sunday, holy day and those few feasts which supplant the Sunday if they should fall on that day.

The structure is simple. The theme for each liturgical celebration is stated. Each reading is summarized with its main thought brought forward, including the Responsorial Psalm. Finally, there is a thought for the day which can serve as a meditation point for the liturgy and the ensuing week.

The liturgy is so developed that two main thoughts are brought forth. In the vast majority of liturgies the first and third readings are related, giving one thought. Usually the first reading is from the Old Testament, although in the Easter Cycle the Book of Acts is used. The third reading is always from the Gospels. The second reading brings us a thought from the various Epistles. The Responsorial Psalm echoes the theme of the Mass.

The old adage that we only get out of something what we put into it is very true of the liturgy. Our Sunday celebrations will enrich us according to our preparation. The Sunday liturgy should be the center of our spiritual life, the manna that keeps us spiritually alive week to week. It is fitting that we spend at least a brief time, preferably on Saturday, for consideration of the next day's liturgical action, to learn what the Church is saying to us through the Word of God, and making ourselves ready to receive it not only joyfully but meaningfully as well. The following calendar sets the liturgical cycles. The liturgies are given in full in Cycle A. If in the other two cycles a liturgy is repeated, reference is made to the page where it first appears. The liturgical year begins on the First Sunday of Advent.

Liturgical Cycles

1984 A	1985 B	1986 C
1987 A	1988 B	1989 C
1990 A	1991 B	1992 C
1993 A	1994 B	1995 C
1996 A	1997 B	1998 C
1999 A	2000 B	2001 C

Year A

Nativity Cycle

First Sunday of Advent   < **A**

Theme: Today on the first Sunday of the liturgical year, the Church turns our attention to the coming of Christ. Actually, we commemorate three comings: His physical coming in Bethlehem; His daily coming among us through neighbor, Church and sacraments; and finally His second coming in final judgment.

First Reading (Is 2:1-5): Isaiah looks forward to the reign of God, when all nations will worship one Lord. When that time comes, war will have ended and no nation will ever again go to war with another.

Responsorial Psalm (Ps 122): This psalm was sung by pilgrims as they made their way to the temple in Jerusalem.

Second Reading (Rom 13:11-14): In a short but poetic and powerful passage, Paul exhorts the Romans to be ready to meet Christ, prepared to have their deeds exposed to the light of day. He contrasts Isaiah's message with his own by telling his Christians to put on the armor of light.

Third Reading (Mt 24:37-44): Matthew is concerned with the destruction that will come with the end of the world and the need for all men to be ready. He quotes Jesus, who compares what happened in the time of Noah with what is to come. The implication is that despite warnings men will again be unconcerned right up to the time of destruction. The words of Jesus are not a threat but a warning to all who will but listen.

Thought for the Day: For most men and women in the world today, war has been almost a continuous experience. Such an experience should make a prudent person very wary of worldly values. Our only confidence can be in Christ and no other.

Second Sunday of Advent < A

Theme: Preparation for the coming of the Lord is the theme of the Advent liturgy. To help us prepare ourselves the Church calls upon the great messianic prophet, Isaiah, and Christ's forerunner, John the Baptist.

First Reading (Is 11:1-10): Isaiah was a prophet whose vision went beyond the Jews to the acceptance of the Messiah by the Gentiles. It was a radical thought for his time. In today's reading he projects this thought in colorful imagery that has the Messiah uniting the most unlikely opposites.

Responsorial Psalm (Ps 72): A prophetic psalm which, while having David in mind, applies to the Christ who will unite all the tribes of earth in justice and under His own divine rule.

Second Reading (Rom 15:4-9): Paul reminds the Romans to live in harmony one with another. Christ gave the example in accepting each one of them as His brothers and sisters.

Third Reading (Mt 3:1-12): John the Baptist warns those who have come to him seeking salvation that being a Jew is not enough. The conversion of a man must be from within. He prophesies of the Christ, who will separate the saved and the damned.

Thought for the Day: While John gives testimony of the nearness of Christ, Isaiah describes Him in terms that are unequaled. Jesus has been especially blessed by His Father, so much so that John feels unworthy even to carry His sandals. Yet this same Jesus who awed the prophets with His majesty is our brother and confidant. It is a gift we can never fully comprehend.

Third Sunday of Advent < A

Theme: The liturgy today answers a question that has concerned people of many ages: Who is Jesus?

First Reading (Is 35:1-6, 10): Although God had many times shown His mercy towards them, the Israelites thought of God in terms of justice and wrath. Isaiah, however, sees the Messiah as a God of love and concern. In this passage he prophesies that the Christ will be a savior and healer.

Responsorial Psalm (Ps 146): This psalm carries forward the idea presented by Isaiah. We sing of God's concern for the weak, the needy, the lowly.

Second Reading (Jas 5:7-10): The apostle James in his letter uses the harshest terms in Scripture in condemning the insensitive rich. Then he suddenly changes direction and exhorts his readers to patience. In accordance with the Advent theme, he reminds them that the judge is at the gate, that Christ will come again and make all things right.

Third Reading (Mt 11:2-11): While John is in prison, his disciples approach Christ and pointedly ask: "Who are you?" Jesus does not answer them directly but points to His actions: His works of healing and curing, His miracles, and above all the message He preaches and its audience. Indirectly, He is telling them that He is the one who is fulfilling the prophecies of Isaiah. The proof of His identity is in His works.

Thought for the Day: No man can truly know himself without knowing who Jesus is. Whether we wish it or not, we are all linked to the identity of Christ. Sooner or later, if we wish to fulfill ourselves and know our own identity, we must ask the same question as John's disciples. The answer is present in the Scriptures.

Fourth Sunday of Advent   < A

Theme: The liturgy today closes the season of Advent preparation on a note that reminds us of the proximity of Christmas. "A virgin is with child," the liturgy tells us, "and his name is 'God is with us.' "

First Reading (Is 7:10-14): This is Isaiah's most famous and direct prophecy of the Christ. King Ahaz is worried about keeping his throne. Isaiah tells him not to trouble God about such a minor matter, because God has promised a messiah from the house of David. The sign by which all men will know is he will be born of a virgin.

Responsorial Psalm (Ps 24): Pilgrim hymn sung entering

3

the Temple, a reminder that Jesus is about to enter the world. **Second Reading** (Rom 1:1-7): Paul opens his letter to the Romans by describing the Gospel he is preaching — one which God promised through the prophets and has come to fulfillment in Jesus. Jesus receives humanity through his descent from David but through the Spirit is the Son of God.

Third Reading (Mt 1:18-25): The Church prepares us for the immediate birth of Jesus by recounting how Joseph accepted Mary, even though she was already with child. Matthew reminds us that these events took place this way so that the prophecy of Isaiah found in the First Reading might be fulfilled. Joseph was a man of faith who did not question God but did His bidding even though he did not understand it.

Thought for the Day: The Incarnation is the most stupendous act in human history. It is one that the wisest man can never fully understand or appreciate. Yet the simplest person can comprehend the love of God for us as shown through a mother and child. In the person of Jesus Christ, the human and divine meet and He becomes at once both our brother and our God.

Christmas (Midnight Mass), Dec. 25   <   A,B,C

Theme: A great light has been shown us, sings Isaiah. Paul tells us God's grace has been revealed. The angelic host reminds us why we are here: "A Savior has been born to you; He is Christ the Lord."

First Reading (Is 9:2-7): Of all the prophets none saw more clearly the promised Messiah than Isaiah. Although he sees a child born to us, what marvelous and prescient titles he lays upon the child: Wonder-Counselor, God-Hero, Father-Forever, Prince of Peace.

Responsorial Psalm (Ps 96): The presence of the Lord is cause for all the world to rejoice.

Second Reading (Ti 2:11-14): Paul had installed Titus as bishop of the Church on Crete. He reminds him that Christ has been revealed as God's living grace, source of salvation for all. It is Paul's testimony to the divinity of Jesus.

Third Reading (Lk 2:1-14): The Gospel is the familiar account of the birth of Jesus Christ. It is significant that the Fa-

4

ther's message of His Son's birth is not given to the noble and rich but to simple shepherds guarding their flocks.

Thought for the Day: What you have done this night is very symbolic. You came out of a dark world into the light of Christ. You will go out once more into the darkness of a world that pays little heed to the Prince of Peace. But the light born here this night must burn always in your hearts.

Christmas (Dawn Mass)   <   A,B,C

Theme: The Midnight Mass focuses on our Savior's birth, both glorious and humble. The dawn Mass turns towards the effects of that birth on each of us.

First Reading (Is 2:11-12): In the words of Isaiah, victory has been achieved. The waiting is over and joy can be proclaimed. The whole world echoes God's edict for Jerusalem: "Look, your Savior comes." God's highway to Jerusalem becomes a way of pilgrimage for all nations.

Responsorial Psalm (Ps 97): Joy over the dawning of light for the just.

Second Reading (Ti 3:4-7): Paul interrupts his instruction to Titus to go into doctrinal rapture. In a parallel he has never used before, he calls God the Father and the Son our Savior. What it has taken a long time for Paul to say in Romans, he now explains succinctly. To the person of faith comes salvation through baptism and renewal of the Holy Spirit, promises of eternal life.

Third Reading (Lk 2:15-20): The Dawn Mass continues the Gospel of midnight. The shepherds react with haste, like Mary at her angelic visitation. Both they and she were given signs. Mary was given the sign of Elizabeth's son. The shepherds were sent to a newborn babe — their Messiah and Savior. Their reaction is one of praise, while Mary ponders the marvels of God in her heart.

Thought for the Day: The Church invites us to reflect with Mary on the great mystery. With Mary we are invited to bring God's light to the world. It is a mission which never ceases and which continually finds new forms of expression. In the quiet joy of Christmas, Christ is born again in the Church. The question each of us must ask is: Is Christ born again in me?

Christmas (Mass during the day)   < A,B,C

Theme: The Midnight Mass was the historical recounting of the birth of Jesus; the dawn Mass, its effect on mankind. This Mass considers the theological implications.

First Reading (Is 52:7-10): While Isaiah here is speaking of the restoration of Zion and the return of exiles, the real good news is that salvation is in Jesus Christ and as a result of His birth salvation is offered to all on earth.

Responsorial Psalm (Ps 98): The psalmist carries forward the theme of Isaiah.

Second Reading (Heb 1:1-16): The time of God speaking through His prophets has passed and God now speaks to us directly through His Son. In this beautiful incarnational hymn, Paul identifies Jesus with the Father, worthy of worship by all creation.

Third Reading (Jn 1:1-18): In the magnificent opening of his Gospel, John summarizes the incarnational theology of Jesus Christ, who existed from the beginning and is one with the Father, too often unrecognized by the world. Jesus' great gift to us is that we too can become children of God.

Thought for the Day: Birthdays are happy events. The most important birthday ever in the world is today — not simply because of the sentiment of the manger but because it offers eternal life to every man, woman and child.

Holy Family
(Sunday in Christmas Octave)   < A,B,C

Theme: Love is the basic element that forms the Christian family; love between husband and wife, children and parents. That love will come if whatever we do, we do in the name of the Lord Jesus Christ.

First Reading (Sir 3:2-5, 12-14): Ben Sira, also known as Ecclesiasticus, is known for his writings in praise of wisdom, which he simply interprets as obedience to the Lord. Out of this obedience he makes a commentary on the Fourth Commandment (Honor your father and mother). He tells us that God places great importance on the honor rendered parents and that respect given them will atone for many sins and offenses. **Responsorial Psalm** (Ps 128): In this wisdom psalm the word "fear" is used as it is in Sirach, as meaning "obedience" or "reverence."

Second Reading (Col 3:12-21): Paul states the basic theme of today's liturgy: Love unites all other virtues and makes them perfect. He applies this virtue to family life and shows how by making love a living thing, proper family relationships will be established.

Third Reading (Mt 2:13-15, 19-23): While this Gospel sets up a problem for Scripture scholars in quoting a text ("He shall be called a Nazorean") which can be found in none of the known prophets, this need not concern us because it is incidental to the main point of the Gospel of how God and the child's parents took care of the Son. There is also a symbolism in the Gospel. Just as the main event in Jewish history was the Exodus from Egypt, so the infant Christ goes there to return to become the leader of His people.

Thought for the Day: In the language of today, family life is where it is at. The relationships between husband and wife, parents and children, are ones that touch the lives of all of us. Shelves upon shelves of books have been written about family life, but in today's liturgy the fundamental principles are set down. We should meditate on them at length.

Mary, Mother of God (Jan. 1)   < A,B,C

Theme: Vatican II is responsible for today's feast. Formerly called the Circumcision and then the Holy Name of Jesus, now because of the emphasis of the Council it is the Feast of Mary, the Mother of God.

First Reading (Nm 6:22-27): An echo of the Feast of the Holy Name is found in this reading from Numbers. So sacred was God's name, Yahweh, that the term "Lord" was used in its place. This use is dramatized as the triple blessing progresses: 1) the preservation of the people, 2) prosperity under God's gaze and favor, 3) and finally the greatest blessing — God's peace.

Responsorial Psalm (Ps 67): A call for God's blessing upon us.

7

Second Reading (Gal 4:4-7): This is an important theological reading. God's salvation comes as a free gift to those who accept the Gospel in faith. Because of Jesus, we do not stand off from God as did the Jews, but we can call God "Abba," Father. As sons we are heirs of God's kingdom. This is a tremendous theological truth, the consequences of which we cannot even imagine. We no longer belong to the minority of the Old Testament but have reached our majority in the New Covenant established by Jesus.

Third Reading (Lk 2:16-21): A Christmas Gospel is repeated. As the angel requested, they name the child Jesus, Yeshua in Hebrew, which means "salvation" or, as popularly understood, "God saves." Heir to Abraham through circumcision, Jesus is the salvation of the Father.

Thought for the Day: The heart of today's feast is Mary's unique relationship with her Divine Son. Her salvation came through the faith she showed in bearing her child. All her privileges come from her divine motherhood.

Epiphany (Sunday between Jan. 2-8)   <   A,B,C

Theme: The word *epiphania* means "a showing" or "revelation." Today's feast marks the revelation or showing of the infant Christ to the world. It is a great missionary feast, whose significance is that Christ is meant for the salvation of all everywhere.

First Reading (Is 60:1-6): Isaiah sees in the Messiah a light that will shine forth from Jerusalem and pierce the darkness of the whole world. People from all nations will approach the light, bringing gifts for their Savior.

Responsorial Psalm (Ps 72): The image of Isaiah is carried forward by the psalmist, who sings that every nation on earth will adore the true God.

Second Reading (Eph 3:2, 5-6): Paul speaks very bluntly and openly to the Ephesians, telling them that God's secret plan is that Jesus Christ should belong to all peoples. Jesus did not come solely to save the Jews but to make every person in every part of the world co-heirs with the Jews. This secret was the motivation for Paul's apostolate.

8

Third Reading (Mt 2:1-12): The Gospel today recounts the familiar story of the Magi. What is important is not the actual details of men coming from great distances but the revelation of Christ to the world beyond Judea. Matthew's point is that Christ is the revelation to all nations and that people of every nationality must give Him the worship that is due the Son of God.

Thought for the Day: It has been said that our quest in life is a search for truth. Indeed, truth is the object of our intellect. For some, truth is perceived wrongly and imperfectly. Today's liturgy points out that the real object of truth is God, made known to us in the person of Jesus Christ. To understand Jesus is to know the Father. Our resolve should be to learn all we can about Jesus through study of the New Testament and meditation on its contents.

The Baptism of the Lord
(Sunday after Epiphany)   <   A,B,C

Theme: After Jesus was baptized by John, God's favor descended upon Him in the person of the Holy Spirit, visible evidence to the prophecy of Isaiah. Baptism gave sacramental character to the mission of Christ.

First Reading (Is 42:1-4, 6-7): This great prophecy of Christ sees the Redeemer as a light to all nations, ending spiritual blindness. This chosen one will call all to justice, which is the real foundation for true peace.

Responsorial Psalm (Ps 29): The psalmist uses a favorite image of Old Testament writers: the voice of God heard in thunder. He likens God to a thunderstorm coming in over the Holy Land from the Mediterranean Sea, bringing refreshment to a parched land with its rain. It is mindful of the voice of God speaking at the baptism of His Son.

Second Reading (Acts 10:34-38): Peter sees the public life of Jesus beginning with His baptism by John, but he also points out the role of the Holy Spirit, whom he sees directing that mission. This is Peter's last missionary discourse in Scripture.

Third Reading (Mk 1:7-11): Mark makes use of John only to confirm the mission of Jesus. The Father uses the words of the psalmist, and the Holy Spirit appears in visible form. There

9

is great symbolism in this short passage. Christ is the new Israel coming from the waters of the new Exodus. This beginning of a new age is signed with the presence of the Spirit in visible form.

Thought for the Day: We should consider the meaning of our own baptism, through which we were initiated into the Christian family with all the responsibilities that initiation implies. Do we communicate to others the Christian message which we received?

Paschal Cycle

First Sunday of Lent   < A

Theme: The liturgy today is the story of harsh reality — mankind's basic weakness and its redemption through Jesus Christ. While Lent is a time for penance, it is also a season for optimism. By ourselves we can do nothing but get into trouble, yet with Christ all things become possible for us.

First Reading (Gn 2:7-9, 3:1-7): This is the story of man's creation and his fall. Some modernists today attempt to reduce this portion of the Bible to the realm of allegory or myth. But the author is telling us the story of a real man and woman, created by God and enjoying a blessed state with Him. Because of free will, Adam chose to offend God and lost the special gifts given him and his descendants.

Responsorial Psalm (Ps 51): An acknowledgment of our own sinfulness.

Second Reading (Rom 5:12-19): In this important reading Paul makes a contrasting parallel between Adam and Christ. Through Adam sin entered the world and man inherited his fallen nature. Through Christ grace was restored to us and His sacrifice is sufficient for all people of all times.

Third Reading (Mt 4:1-11): This again is a parallel scriptural reading. The Israelites were tested in the desert during their long exodus from Egypt. In this Gospel Matthew shows Christ's own testing in the desert, at the end of which the Father sent angels with His heavenly manna. Before that Christ had to endure the threefold temptation of Satan — to His flesh, to worldly power, and to His own esteem. The devil cleverly uses Scripture for his own purpose.

Thought for the Day: The Church offers us today the choice between the old Adam and the new Adam and the assurance that God's grace is greater than any temptation or sin. Although evil and sin seem so powerful in the world today, the Church reminds us that they were conquered once by Christ and will be conquered by Him once again. This is our Lenten optimism.

Second Sunday of Lent   <   A

Theme: No sacrifice is too great to follow Christ. We must obey the Father's command: "This is my beloved son. Listen to him" (Lk 9:35).

First Reading (Gn 12:1-4): The call of Abraham is recounted. He is commanded by God to leave the land of his family and go to a place God will show him. In full trust in God, Abraham does as God asks him. This reading gives the example of the way we should follow Christ.

Responsorial Psalm (Ps 33): A hymn of trust in God. It is an echo of Abraham's response and an example for our own conduct.

Second Reading (2 Tm 1:8-10): Paul encourages his disciple Timothy to remain strong in his faith, despite all hardships. Like Abraham, God has called us into a new life, this time the life of the Gospels. This call comes not from any merit of our own but simply through God's grace.

Third Reading (Mt 17:1-9): Matthew recounts for us today the story of the Transfiguration. It was a revelation on the part of the Father to Peter, John and James so that their faith could be made stronger for the trials that lay ahead and which were to climax in the passion and death of Christ. Once again we find the scriptural symbolism both of the mountain being the meeting place between God and man, and of the Father appearing in the form of a cloud. The essence of the reading is the command of the Father to hear and obey the Son.

Thought for the Day: As we progress into Lent, the Church

11

calls for greater unity with Jesus. God is at work among men, and in this revelation to man the Father confirms the Sonship of Jesus. It will be this Son who will be the means of our own salvation and who will share with us His divine life.

Third Sunday of Lent < A

Theme: At first the theme of today's readings seems to be water. But they really only concern water insofar as it is a symbol of life. The living water we need is Christ.

First Reading (Ex 17:3-7): When the people of Israel suffer from thirst in their exodus from Egypt, Moses saves them by drawing water from a rock. It is a miracle of God's presence among the children of Israel, a sign of His lasting care.

Responsorial Psalm (Ps 95): This is a hymn of faith with a reminder of past doubts of God's protection.

Second Reading (Rom 5:1-2, 5-8): God has proven His love for us through the death of His Son, Jesus. Now the Holy Spirit pours God's love into us if we will but let it operate within ourselves.

Third Reading (Jn 4:5-42): The story of Jesus at the well with the Samaritan woman is the subject for sermons on many different topics — baptism, marriage, faith, the will of God, to mention but a few. Yet the most important element of the story is Christ's own revelation of himself as the Messiah.

Thought for the Day: "He told me everything I ever did." This was reason for belief by the Samaritan woman. The response of this woman was one of faith. Through Baptism we were initiated into Christ, but we only grow in Christ by a present and active faith.

Fourth Sunday of Lent < A

Theme: God does not act without reason, and from the dawn of history His saving plan was in effect. Today we see two more stages in that plan: the calling of David and the restoration of sight to the young man born blind, an act which symbolizes the spiritual sight of the Christian.

First Reading (1 Sm 16:1, 6-7, 10-13): The selection of David to lead Israel plays an important role in salvation history, for it is from his lineage that the Savior will come. David was Israel's greatest king, the one against whom all others would be measured.

Responsorial Psalm (Ps 23): This is probably the most beautiful and best known of all of the psalms. Although the psalmist compares God to a shepherd, this Shepherd is one with whom he would dwell forever.

Second Reading (Eph 5:8-14): Paul looks upon paganism as a place of darkness to which only Christ can give light. He urges his readers to be productive in those things which the light of Christ gives.

Third Reading (Jn 9:1-41): Christ uses this miracle of restoring sight to a blind man to condemn an even greater evil, spiritual blindness. The waters of Siloam are symbolic of the waters of baptism.

Thought for the Day: Lent is a particular time for reconciliation with God. Our reconciliation begins with his baptism, but baptism must lead to belief which is expressed in action. The blind man's confession of faith must always be active in our own lives.

Fifth Sunday of Lent   < A

Theme: The heart of today's liturgy lies in the promise of resurrection. Eternal life is God's plan for us, but unfortunately one is free to reject this great gift.

First Reading (Ez 37:12-14): It is the role of Ezekiel to give confidence to the exiled Israelites, whom he pictures as dried bones awaiting the resurrection. He reassures the exiles that all of God's promises will be kept.

Responsorial Psalm (Ps 130): The Church has traditionally associated this psalm, the *De Profundis* (Out of the Depths), with the anguish of the dead awaiting resurrection in Christ. Although it is a call for aid, it is also a prayer of faith in God.

Second Reading (Rom 8:8-11): St. Paul reminds us that the real death is to be in sin and separated from the Spirit. As long as we live in the Spirit, we will have life within us.

Third Reading (Jn 11:1-45): There is enough in this Sunday's

Gospel of the resurrection of Lazarus for a score of homilies. It prefigures Christ's own resurrection. It shows Christ's power over death. It answers Martha's objection that the resurrection will take place on the last day: Jesus reminds her that He is the resurrection and those who believe in Him will live even though they have suffered bodily death.

Thought for the Day: There is a dire warning in the liturgy of this day. At our death we will know whether we shall truly live or truly die. The real death is to be cut off from God for all eternity. He who lives the life of the Lord will then fully understand the meaning of the words: "I am the resurrection and the life."

Passion Sunday   < A,B,C

Theme: Lent draws to a close on a false note of triumph. The blessing and distribution of palms recalls Our Lord's exultant entry into Jerusalem for the last time. The Third Reading, however, reminds us that in less than a week these same streets will be stained with His blood.

First Reading (Is 50:4-7): God's prophets were not always honored but, like Isaiah, often abused. In his suffering Isaiah prefigures Christ and becomes His voice.

Responsorial Psalm (Ps 22): A development of the Isaiah theme. This psalm of prophecy sees Our Lord abandoned and mocked, His body pierced, His garments divided. Yet there is also trust here.

Second Reading (Phil 2:6-11): In a conciseness that could only be inspired by the Holy Spirit, Paul in a few words summarizes the humanity and divinity of Jesus, His suffering and victory, all in the firm faith that Jesus is Lord.

Year A

Third Reading (Mt 26.14-27,66): Matthew shows Christ suffering silently for the sins of the world. He emphasizes the claim of Jesus to be God's Son. As a result, when Jesus dies, even the earth through its quaking protests the fact; the rending of the temple veil proclaims the new order. In contrast to the Jewish

14

leaders, even the Roman soldiers say, "Clearly this was the Son of God!"

Year B

Third Reading (Mk 14:1 — 15:47): Mark's account of the Passion is a story of failure: the betrayal of Judas, the slumbering disciples, the denial of Peter, the abandonment of the apostles. Yet through it all Jesus remains a majestic figure — the persecuted man with complete trust in Yahweh.

Year C

Third Reading (Lk 22:14 — 23:56): Luke's account of the Passion is a story of victory. The lengthy details of Jesus making His way to Jerusalem are climaxed with His triumph on the cross. In derision Pilate placed a sign over the head of Jesus: "This is the king of the Jews," but His kingdom was not of this world. It was to paradise He took the good thief.

Thought for the Day: During the rest of this week the Church wishes us to unite ourselves closely with the events in the last week in the life of Jesus. Only by suffering with Him can we fittingly celebrate the triumph of Easter.

Easter Sunday   < A,B,C

Theme: The heart of today's liturgy is in John's description of when he found the tomb empty: "He saw and he believed." It was the resurrection of Christ that sealed the faith of His followers. Unless the Lord is risen our faith is in vain.

First Reading (Acts 10:34, 37-43): This is Peter's final recorded sermon in Acts. He gives the reasons for his vocation. He has been a witness to all that he preaches, including the resurrection of Christ. He must proclaim that fact to the whole world.

Responsorial Psalm (Ps 118): The Lord has triumphed. The stone rejected by the builders has become the cornerstone.

Second Reading (Col 3:1-4): In baptism we were buried to all that is worldly and from baptism we rose anew in Christ. The victories or ills of life mean nothing because our final glory is in Christ.

15

Alternate Second Reading (1 Cor 5:6-8): If we are to be faithful to Christ our Passover, we must rid ourselves of all that is worldly.

Third Reading (Jn 20:1-9): John tells precisely what he and Peter saw on the day of Resurrection, even to the detail of one cloth out of place. Although Christ had predicted His resurrection, His disciples did not understand. Although John does not even now understand, he makes an act of faith, an example to us all.

Alternate Third Reading (Mt 28:1-10): Jesus appears to the holy women and tells them He will meet His disciples in Galilee. It was there He began His mission and it is there He will end it.

Alternate Third Reading for Evening Mass (Lk 24:13-35): In his account of the happenings on the road to Emmaus, Luke gives a eucharistic cast to the first Easter Sunday. Although Jesus is risen, He is always with us in the form of bread.

Thought for the Day: Although the liturgy relates the facts surrounding the resurrection of Jesus, what is behind them is the active power of God as present in Jesus. It is not a dead Jesus we consider today but the God-man who is truly active and present among us at this very moment. Jesus is not only risen but He is here now, this very moment. All the values of the world are changed by our belief in the Resurrection.

Second Sunday of Easter   < A

Theme: Belief in Christ and all that He taught is the dominant note of these Easter readings, best summarized by Thomas' profession of faith: "My Lord and my God!"

First Reading (Acts 2:42-47): Luke describes the communal life of the early Church in Jerusalem and its growth. What is significant here is the distinction made between ordinary communal meals and the ceremony of prayer and the breaking of bread, the early name for the eucharistic sacrifice.

Responsorial Psalm (Ps 118): A hymn of thanksgiving for the Resurrection.

Second Reading (1 Pt 1:3-9): Christian life draws its strength and validity from the resurrection of Jesus Christ. This is the message Peter gives in opening his first letter. He also

16

sees in Christ's resurrection the promise of our own redemption.

Third Reading (Jn 20:19-31): John now brings his Gospel to a close. He has spoken of Christ and His love for us, proven by many miracles. The greatest of all His miracles was His resurrection. Christ appears to His disciples, locked behind closed doors. He confirms them in the Spirit and establishes the Sacrament of Penance. John emphasizes what has happened by recounting Jesus' reappearance a week later to receive Thomas' belated confession of faith. Having thus proved his thesis, John closes, wishing all his readers eternal life because of their own faith.

Thought for the Day: While today's readings center about the Resurrection, they confirm central truths of our Faith: the Holy Spirit, the Catholic Church and the forgiveness of sin through the Sacrament of Penance. Christ's words to His apostles specifically give them power to forgive or retain sin, a distinctive mark of the Catholic Church.

Third Sunday of Easter   < A

Theme: The liturgy today is transitory, drawing on the prophets of the Old Covenant to prove the validity of Christ's claims and the ultimate proof, His resurrection.

First Reading (Acts 2:14, 22-28): Luke reconstructs for us here a portion of the first public sermon in the new Church, Peter's discourse on Pentecost. In this selection Peter unites the New and Old Covenant by declaring the credentials of Christ to be proven by His own miracles, but also by calling on the prophecy of Israel's greatest and most respected king, David.

Responsorial Psalm (Ps 16): A repetition of Peter's theme with hope in our personal resurrection.

Second Reading (1 Pt 1:17-21): This reading follows that of last Sunday. Peter goes on to remind us that we have gained heaven not as the result of the Old Covenant or any worldly accomplishments but solely by the blood of Christ, on which no human value can be set. The Power that raised Christ from the dead must be the motivation of our own lives.

Third Reading (Lk 24:13-35): This is the familiar story of the disciples from Emmaus and their recognition of the risen

Lord. But the point here is that the disciples should not have been surprised by the events of the past few days; it had all clearly been diagramed for them by the Old Testament prophets and foretold by Jesus. Despite all this evidence, it was only in the breaking of the bread that they finally recognized the risen Lord.

Thought for the Day: We are all much like the disciples from Emmaus. Not only the testimony of the Old Covenant but all that of the New is available to us. How seldom we reflect on it. How little influence it has on our daily acts. We can wonder if even the risen Christ appeared to us, would it make any great difference in how we live each day?

Fourth Sunday of Easter < A

Theme: The idea of Christ as shepherd is echoed throughout today's liturgy. It was Christ who redeemed us and now through His resurrection He has become the gate of the sheepfold wherein all humanity is joined to His Father.

First Reading (Acts 2:14, 36-41): Peter concludes his sermon of Pentecost day by proclaiming to the house of Israel that the Messiah has not only come but has been put to death by Israel. Now salvation is offered to all peoples through baptism in the name of the Lord Jesus Christ. Over three thousand people accept the invitation and are added to the house of the Lord.

Responsorial Psalm (Ps 23): This great psalm of trust is one of the most popular of David's compositions. It is a complete acceptance of the Lord as shepherd.

Second Reading (1 Pt 2:20-25): We have been spiritually healed and made whole through the sufferings of Christ. Before we met Christ we were like wandering sheep, but having accepted His teachings, we can now endure things that before were impossible.

Third Reading (Jn 10:1-10): Jesus compares himself to the hypocritical leaders of Israel by picturing himself as the true shepherd. When His hearers fail to understand His allegory, He speaks more directly, saying that the leaders of Israel are false shepherds who will only lead them to destruction. Only His own teaching will give them fullness of life.

Thought for the Day: If we are to have full life in God, it is a relationship so intimate and so rich in love on the part of God that it demands the same response from each of us. Although the liturgy speaks to each of us directly, it is clear that God's message is meant for all humanity.

Fifth Sunday of Easter   < A

Theme: The work of the Church must always go forward, but it is a work in which everyone must participate according to his or her state in life. Priests and those in orders have special roles, but the laity must also contribute and not just receive.

First Reading (Acts 6:1-7): Luke continues his narration of the formation of the early Church. Today he recounts the selection and ordination of the first deacons, among whom is Stephen, who will become the first martyr.

Responsorial Psalm (Ps 33): A hymn of praise to God with the congregation expressing their trust in Him.

Second Reading (1 Pt 2:4-9): This is an important reading because Peter speaks of the royal priesthood of which the laity is a part. This is not the sacramental priesthood, for which ordination is necessary; but as members of the Mystical Body all of the laity have a share in the priesthood of Jesus Christ, the cornerstone of our beliefs.

Third Reading (Jn 14:1-12): Humanity has always been puzzled by the question: What is God like? Being pure spirit and the superlative of every good thing, our finite minds can never comprehend His infinite majesty and greatness. Yet we can know God and in a very simple way. Today's Gospel gives us the formula when Philip asks this very question. Christ replies directly: "Whoever has seen me has seen the Father." By knowing Christ, we know God the Father.

Thought for the Day: Jesus is the way to God. He states this very clearly. Jesus reveals himself to us through His Gospels and through His people. If we love Christ, we will truly try to study and learn all we can about Him. It would be very sad if when we finally meet Him in our judgment He should say to us: "I have been with you all this time and you still do not know me."

Sixth Sunday of Easter   < A

Theme: The liturgy now begins to look forward to Pentecost. The readings today are concerned with the Holy Spirit and His necessary roles in our lives. The Spirit is Our Lord's special and necessary gift to His followers, a fact that the apostles clearly realized after Pentecost.

First Reading (Acts 8:5-8, 14-17): The deacon Philip preaches the Gospel in Samaria and makes many converts. To bestow the Sacrament of Confirmation on these new Christians, Peter and John come from Jerusalem. It is evident that even at this early stage of Church development, certain roles belonged solely to its bishops.

Responsorial Psalm (Ps 66): One of the most beautiful and exuberant psalms is today used as a hymn of praise and confidence.

Second Reading (1 Pt 3:15-18): Being a Christian in the early Church was not easy and there was both subtle and direct persecution. Peter tells his readers how to meet this test to their faith and reminds them that Christ suffered the same fate but lives eternally in the Spirit.

Third Reading (Jn 14:15-21): Jesus is preparing His disciples for His departure. He promises that He will not leave them alone but will send the Holy Spirit who guides the Church today and keeps it in the truth.

Thought for the Day: The Spirit comes to the Catholic in a special way in the Sacrament of Confirmation, which completes the Sacrament of Baptism. We are expected to cooperate with the special gifts which come to us in confirmation, to nurture them within us and make them grow. Only in this way can we become mature and adult Christians.

Ascension of Our Lord
(Thursday of Sixth Week of Easter)   < A,B,C

Theme: Christ returns to the Father and eternal glory as King of the universe. His ascension into heaven is the promise of our own ascension to be in His company forever.

First Reading (Acts 1:1-11): The Book of Acts opens with a

20

summary of Christ's last forty days on earth, culminating in His ascension into heaven. There is a promise of a Second Coming but it is hidden in the mystery of the Father. Meanwhile, the Church of Christ is to be carried to the ends of the earth.

Responsorial Psalm (Ps 47): A joyous acclamation of God in heaven.

Second Reading (Eph 1:17-23): Jesus has now become the mystery of the Church, reconciling Jew and Gentile. Because He fulfilled His Father's will, Jesus has been enthroned and the power of God now acts through Him.

Year A

Third Reading (Mk 16:15-20): Matthew does not end his Gospel with a description of the Ascension. Instead he chooses to close his work on a mountain in Galilee with Christ's great command to His apostles: Go, teach, baptize. Jesus promises to be in His Church until the end of time.

Year B

Third Reading (Mk 16:15-20): After Jesus commands His apostles to undertake a universal mission of salvation, He is lifted up to the right hand of the Father, whence He shall reign. The apostles obey His command and take the Gospel to the world, the Lord working in them.

Year C

Third Reading (Lk 24:46-53): Luke places the scene of the Ascension in the outskirts of Bethany. Jesus speaks of himself as the fulfillment of the messianic prophecies. From Jerusalem His Gospel will go out to all the world. Luke leaves the carrying out of this command for his next work, the Book of Acts.

Thought for the Day: As Christians, we must never lose sight of the mission Jesus placed on His Church. By baptism we are dedicated to mission. As the new Code of Canon Law reminds us (Canon 204), we "are called, each according to his or her particular condition, to exercise the mission which God entrusted to the Church to fulfill in the world."

Seventh Sunday of Easter < A

Theme: On this last Sunday before Pentecost, the Church seeks to make us ready for the historical coming of the Spirit and His revitalization of the infant Church. Pentecost is not only the remembrance of an act of history but also a reminder of our own personal life in the Spirit.

First Reading (Acts 1:12-14): This reading puts the apostles back into the upper room of the Last Supper, where they are awaiting the coming of the Holy Spirit. It is interesting to note the importance Mary was playing in the life of the early Church.

Responsorial Psalm (Ps 27): This is another beautiful psalm in which David pledges to live in the house of the Lord all the days of his life. This prayer should also be our own.

Second Reading (1 Pt 4:13-16): It is a great glory to suffer for being a Christian. Although this reading of Peter is reflective of his own life, it has a particular application to our times, when we live in a secularized world that has little regard for Christianity or its most sacred beliefs.

Third Reading (Jn 17:1-11): This reading is Christ's prayer to His Father. He tells the Father that He has done the work assigned to Him. He has taught His followers that everything comes from the Father, and He has passed on to them all that He has been instructed to give. Now having fulfilled the tasks given Him, Jesus asks for the glory that is rightly His. He has given the Father glory on earth, now He asks for His own glory at the side of the Father.

Thought for the Day: Jesus has made the name and the love of the Father known to each one of us. He has entrusted us with the message given Him by the Father. What is our response? Do we live up to the teachings of Christ? Are we worthy of the sacrifice made for us and the confidence placed in us by Our Lord? The answers will tell us how truly Christian we are.

Pentecost Sunday < A,B,C

Theme: Pentecost is the closing and crowning event of the Easter cycle. Despite the Lord's teaching, His miracles and even His resurrection, the faith of the apostles and disciples was

confused and uncertain. Then, on Pentecost Day with the visible coming of the Holy Spirit, everything fell into place and great missioners were born.

First Reading (Acts 2:1-11): God appeared in the form of fire to seal His covenant with Moses. Now God comes again as fire in the person of the Holy Spirit to confirm His New Law. Transformed, the apostles go forth immediately to preach to men of many nations "the marvels God has accomplished." It is the birth of the new Church.

Responsorial Psalm (Ps 104): It is the Spirit of the Lord that re-creates a new world. This psalm is repeated from yesterday's vigil.

Second Reading (1 Cor 12:3-7, 12-13): Paul, in this counseling of the Church in Corinth, plays down the extraordinary manifestations of the Holy Spirit to point out that the real gift of the Spirit is in the profession of one and the same faith. The Spirit in Paul's view gives unity to the body of Christ, and anything that is divisive is not of the Spirit.

Third Reading (Jn 20:19-23): This reading emphasizes that the mystery of the Resurrection and Pentecost are the same. The Spirit of Jesus is the unity of His Church. It is through this Spirit that the Gospel will be preached to all men and all men in turn will become one in the body of Christ. It is the Spirit of Christ that binds us together and makes us one Church.

Thought for the Day: For a long time, the Holy Spirit seemed to be the forgotten Person of the Blessed Trinity. In recent years there has grown a new understanding and realization of the need for the Spirit not only in our own lives but in renewing the world. The Alleluia hymn ("Come, Holy Spirit, fill the hearts of Your faithful; and kindle in them the fire of Your love") should be our constant prayer.

Trinity Sunday (Sunday after Pentecost)　　< A

Theme: Today is really a feast of love — the love of God for man. St. John's simple description, "God is love," has never been equaled. That love is best exemplified in the Holy Trinity, where Father and Son are united in the love of the Holy Spirit.

First Reading (Ex 34:4-6, 8-9): Although Moses has already

23

received the Ten Commandments, the Jews have deserted God for a golden calf. Moses, at God's direction, goes back up Mt. Sinai with two blank tablets of stone on which God will write again His commandments and His covenant with the people of Israel.

Responsorial Psalm (Dn 3:52-56): This hymn is taken from the canticle in the Book of Daniel which was sung by the three young men who were thrown into the furnace by Nebuchadnezzar. It is a hymn of praise and confidence in God.

Second Reading (2 Cor 13:11-13): The end of this reading is preserved as one of the optional readings that begin the Mass. It is the greeting commemorating the Trinity.

Third Reading (Jn 3:16-18): Jesus clearly proclaims His Sonship to Nicodemus, citing himself as a proof of God's love for us. There is an important qualification laid down: Salvation will come only to those who believe.

Thought for the Day: Many have tried to explain the Trinity but, because it is a mystery, it is beyond the comprehension of our finite minds. The Gospels clearly proclaim the three Persons in God. While not comprehending the mystery, in the spirit of the Gospel we believe and hope for eternal life.

Corpus Christi (Body of Christ)
Sunday after Trinity   < A

Theme: If you do not partake of the Body of Christ, you will have no life in you.

First Reading (Dt 8:2-3, 14-16): The Israelites have grown weary of their long desert wanderings. Moses reminds them of how God has taken care of their essential needs by showering them with bread from heaven and bringing forth water from a rock.

Responsorial Psalm (Ps 147): A song praising God for His particular care of the Israelites.

Second Reading (1 Cor 10:16-17): A reminder by St. Paul that those who share in the Body and Blood of Christ are truly one.

Third Reading (Jn 6:51-58): The miracle of the loaves and fishes was a direct preparation for this discourse of Christ, in which He clearly proclaimed the doctrine of the Eucharist. By partaking of the body and blood of Christ we are joined with Him and the Father. This was a radical and shocking doctrine for the Jews. Many of them refused to accept it, and they turned away from Christ and followed Him no longer. Their rejection of Christ showed that they clearly understood what He was teaching.

Thought for the Day: Just as the Jews could not have sustained life in the desert without the intervention of God in giving them food for the body, so our spiritual life will wither and die without the heavenly food of His Body and Blood, which will sustain us until we are finally joined to Him for eternity.

Ordinary Time

Second Sunday of the Year   < A

Theme: The liturgy today emphasizes the fact that Jesus Christ is God's Chosen One, whose mission is to offer salvation to all on earth. There is a distinct missionary flavor to today's readings.

First Reading (Is 49:3, 5-6): Isaiah is the chief prophet of the Old Testament. It was he who saw more clearly than any other the nature of the Messiah, and he expressed his prophecy in terms of great beauty and imagery. Today we read his record of God's revelation that He will make Christ "a light to the nations, that my salvation may reach to the ends of the earth."

Responsorial Psalm (Ps 40): A song of obedience to the will of God.

Second Reading (1 Cor 1:1-3): Despite the fact that the Church at Corinth was unruly and given to factionalism, the Christians there had a special spot in Paul's heart. He had converted them and looked upon them as his spiritual children, though not always on their best behavior. Sometimes he writes to them in anger, sometimes in sorrow. Today we begin his first existing letter to them. In his greeting he reminds them that they have been called to be holy people. It is a reminder to each one of us too.

Third Reading (Jn 1:29-34): We are reminded of John the Baptist's testimony to Christ every time we attend Mass and hear the words: "This is the Lamb of God who takes away the sins of the world." John declares that he is but an instrument of God to reveal Christ to all Israel. After a mystical experience with the Father, John is able to proclaim without any qualifications that Jesus is "God's Chosen One."

Thought for the Day: Preaching the Gospel is not solely a historical recounting of the life of Christ. It is the proclamation of the Good News which involves God's plan for our salvation. The salvation preached by Christ was directed to all. For this reason our religion cannot be solely personal — a Jesus-and-I relationship. Our religion by its nature must express our own concern for all, and we must in some way work for the salvation of the world as well as our individual salvation.

Third Sunday of the Year   < A

Theme: The message of the liturgy today is very clear: Christ is the light of salvation.

First Reading (Is 8:23 — 9:3): Although Isaiah is speaking against the background of the exile of Israel and the occupation of its land by a foreign power, the messianic interpretation of this great messianic prophet sees the darkness and gloom dispelled by a great light which is the Christ.

Responsorial Psalm (Ps 27): The psalmist clearly states the theme of today's Mass that God is our light and salvation, and he adds an extra note in his reminder that we should love our faith and Church, where we should want to dwell all the days of our lives.

Second Reading (1 Cor 1:10-13,17): The dissensions in the Church in Corinth were a great trial to Paul, the spiritual father of the Church there. In very clear language he tells his converts to stop their quarreling and disputes and remember their essential unity in Christ. There is a practical lesson here for the divisions which exist in Christianity today.

Third Reading (Mt 4:12-23): In prefacing Christ's first call to Peter, James, John and Andrew to become His apostles, Matthew refers back to the prophecy of Isaiah which makes up today's first reading. It is his way of showing that Christ is the promised light and that now the kingdom of God is at hand.

Thought for the Day: There is a great darkness on our land today, and we have become captives of materialistic and anti-Christian forces. God's commandments have been denied, innocent life is no longer held sacred. Indeed, our lot is much like that of the exiled Israelites, but the Light is there for us to discern our way. First we must hear those words: "Reform your lives! The kingdom of heaven is at hand."

Fourth Sunday of Year   < A

Theme: This might be called Beatitude Sunday, for the Beatitudes are the liturgical theme for the Mass.

First Reading (Zep 2:3; 3:12-13): Zephaniah is looked upon as an angry prophet, a prophet of wrath. In today's reading, he tells how to esape God's anger — be humble, be truthful.

Responsorial Psalm (Ps 146): A hymn praising the oppressed and those in need.

Second Reading (1 Cor 1:26-31): Paul tells us that we do not need anything else in the world but Christ, for Christ is our wisdom. The Corinthian converts are not rich or well placed, yet they have been chosen by God to reveal His wisdom before their neighbors. The only thing the Christian should boast of is God himself.

Third Reading (Mt 5:1-12): In the Beatitudes Jesus gives His program in Christian living, a sharp contrast to the values of the world. They come at the beginning of a long sermon which Jesus uses to inaugurate His mission of the kingdom. The Beatitudes sum up the values of Jesus, which are far different than those of the world.

Thought for the Day: While the Beatitudes are concise and direct, they are one of the most difficult parts of the Gospel to understand. They are what the communists once called "pie in the sky." In a world in which making money and gaining power are the values to be sought, Christ's program does seem foolish. Yet God's heart goes always to those in need, not to those who because of riches and might seem sufficient to themselves.

Fifth Sunday of the Year   < A

Theme: Today's liturgy is concerned with the Christian vocation. It is one example. Isaiah tells us we should be like the breaking forth of the dawn. Jesus tells us that we must be a light to the world because it is only by our deeds that men will be drawn to the Father.

First Reading (Is 58:7-10): The corporal works of mercy did not originate with the Church or even Christ. In this reading today we find them mentioned by Isaiah as the way to show the true spirit of religion. Through these works our lives will be as visible as the light at night or the sun of midday. We should not be calling on the Lord for help unless first we have helped others.

Responsorial Psalm (Ps 112): The deeds of a just man speak for themselves. They become a light of example to others.

Second Reading (1 Cor 2:1-5): Paul tells us that the heart of his preaching is very simple: Christ crucified. He realizes that this teaching is contrary to human values and that people can become aware of its value only "by the convincing power of the Spirit."

Third Reading (Mt 5:13-16): In this short but meaningful address to His followers, Christ likens the Christian vocation to salt which gives savor, a city built on a hilltop visible to all, a light shining out to the world. Through our acts, men should be led to give praise to the Father.

Thought for the Day: Many people profess to be Christians and give lip service to the teachings of Christ, but the acid test for all rests in their deeds. The act gives proof of convictions and belief. "By their deeds you shall know them." How do we measure up against this standard?

Sixth Sunday of the Year   < A

Theme: Free will and responsibility. Each one of us has a choice. We can choose eternal life or eternal death.

First Reading (Sir 15:15-20): The blame for sin is not to be laid on the Lord for He hates sin. Each of us has been given the power to choose good or evil and hence reward or punishment.

Once we have acted, the natural consequence will usually follow.

Responsorial Psalm (Ps 119): Happiness is in doing God's will.

Second Reading (1 Cor 2:6-10): We need wisdom, that is, knowledge of God and things divine. This wisdom is a gift to us by the Holy Spirit because the secrets and innermost nature of God are known only by the Holy Spirit.

Third Reading (Mt 5:17-37): In the conclusion of the Sermon on the Mount, Jesus contrasts His New Law with the Old Law. His teaching is not to deny the Old Law, for Christian morality is to be based on the Ten Commandments. But the New Law is not legalistic as was the Old. It is the spirit that counts, rather than mere external observance. Jesus condemns adultery, murder, divorce and swearing to show the difference between old and new.

Thought for the Day: Few people would hestitate to make a choice between life and death by choosing life. Yet it is a choice we can be faced with almost daily as far as our eternal life is concerned. Not everyone who says "Lord, Lord" will enter the kingdom of heaven, but only the ones who do the will of God in their hearts.

Seventh Sunday of the Year   < A

Theme: The readings today might be considered a homily in themselves on the commandment: "You shall love your neighbor as yourself."

First Reading (Lv 9:1-2, 17-18): The Book of Leviticus contains the laws and customs mandated for the Jews. God told the Jews through Moses that they must be holy. This holiness is shown in action by love of God and neighbor.

Responsorial Psalm (Ps 103): We are taught kindness and compassion by God's example.

Second Reading (1 Cor 3:16-23): The wisdom of the world is founded on natural things and can be a hindrance in striving for God's wisdom because its values are completely different. The Gospel the Corinthians heard is what is important, not the ones who preached it.

Third Reading (Mt 5:38-48): In this reading Jesus gives us a homily on the love of neighbor. He has told us in the parable of the Good Samaritan that our neighbor is everyman. Now He tells us we must treat our neighbor as God treats each one of us.

Thought for the Day: Imitating the perfection of God may seem to be an impossible command. Yet Paul tells us that we belong to Christ, hence when we act with Christ nothing is impossible for us. St. Stephen, imitating the forgiveness of his Master, prayed that the sin of his murderers not be held against them. This is an example of the love we must have.

Eighth Sunday of the Year   < A

Theme: God's care is always with us.

First Reading (Is 49:14-15): Although the Jews are exiled in Babylon, they are no more forgotten by God than a mother can forget her child.

Responsorial Psalm (Ps 62): God is our rock and salvation.

Second Reading (1 Cor 4:1-5): Paul is aware of the self-deception that lies within each of us, even himself. Therefore, he leaves his judgment to God, which is all that really counts. God will judge not only deeds but intentions as well.

Third Reading (Mt 6:24-34). This kingdom is not in some distant future but it is here and now. One cannot serve worldly standards and serve God at the same time. This may seem like a most difficult task, but the Providence of God is with us as it is with all creation. God knows what we need. Therefore, we must launch out into the deep and seek the kingdom today.

Thought for the Day: "I will never forget you," promises the Lord. The knowledge that God cares for us, that we are never alone, is essential for growth in the Christian life. Alone we would be lost. The concerns of the world and its values press on us from all sides. Alone they would be too much for us. So we live this day for God with God, worrying not about tomorrow.

Ninth Sunday of the Year   < A

Theme: A person proves his or her words only by deeds. This is what the liturgy tells us today. Moses calls for fidelity to the law, and Jesus in the Gospel speaks quite bluntly.

First Reading (Dt 11:18, 26-28): Moses gives the Israelites either of two choices: wholehearted observance of the law, which will bring a blessing; or failure to keep the law, which will bring a curse. He is foretelling Israel's future.

Responsorial Psalm (Ps 31): God is our refuge and rock.

Second Reading (Rom 3:21-25, 28): This begins a series of Sunday readings from Paul's letter to the Romans, outlining the basic plan of salvation. God's justice works through faith in His Son, Jesus, and faith to Paul is an active commitment to Jesus Christ. A commitment to Jesus Christ presupposes living His teachings.

Third Reading (Mt 7:21-27): Today's reading is the conclusion of the Sermon on the Mount. After outlining His teaching, Jesus declares He does not want lip service but action based on what He has taught. Anyone who does not put it into practice is a foolish person headed for tragedy.

Thought for the Day: All of us have the vague intention of becoming better than we actually are. However, we put off any action and procrastinate. How foolish we would think a man to be who, being warned that a rising river would soon reach his house, did nothing to save his belongings or escape to safety. All of Scripture warns us, but how many do nothing!

Tenth Sunday of the Year   < A

Theme: Today's liturgy is a condemnation of lip-service Christianity. Our religion cannot be legalistic but must come from the heart. It is the spirit of what we do that is important, rather than external forms which we may follow.

First Reading (Hos 6:3-6): Although the Jews were God's Chosen People, time and time again they drifted away from Him. In order to bring them back to His ways, He sent prophets to challenge their consciences. Hosea was such a prophet. In this reading he reminds the Jews that it is what is in their hearts that counts, not the formalities of sacrificial religion.

Responsorial Psalm (Ps 50): Praise of God is better than sacrificing animals.

Second Reading (Rom 4:18-25): In the previous chapter to this reading, Paul has shown that faith is the recipient of God's justice and not the formality of law. Now he gives the example of Abraham, who is the great witness of Old Testament faith. He tells the Romans that their faith in the risen Jesus is the reason they can expect justice from God.

Third Reading (Mt 9:9-13): Matthew gives his own conversion as an example of the justification of faith. Although many Jews considered Matthew a sinner because he did not perfectly obey Mosaic law, Jesus looked into his heart and saw love and repentance and thus called him to be an apostle.

Thought for the Day: Going to Mass on Sunday and observing other Church laws do not really make one a Christian. Observing the legal precepts of our Faith is no guarantee of salvation. This is what the Pharisees did. Our faith is proven by our Christian life and love, not only for God but also for our fellow humans.

Eleventh Sunday of the Year   < A

Theme: God had made a covenant with the Jewish people, and it was through them that He was to be made known to the world. For this reason Christ first directed His mission to the Jews, offering them the first opportunity for salvation — an opportunity the majority were to reject.

First Reading (Ex 19:2-6): God has just rescued the Jews from Egyptian slavery and now renews to Moses His covenant with them. His promise is conditional on their own fidelity.

Responsorial Psalm (Ps 100): This beautiful hymn extols God for adopting us as His people.

Second Reading (Rom 5:6-11): If Christ died for us before we were reconciled to God, it shows God's great love for us. Hence we can be confident of salvation if we do the will of God.

Third Reading (Mt 9:36 — 10:8): Matthew recounts the naming of the Twelve Apostles and Christ's command that His teachings should first be preached to the Jews themselves. They are to tell the Jews that the reign of God is at hand.

Thought for the Day: Jesus begins His mission to the Jews because of the covenant His Father has made with them. At the same time He proclaims that He has come for the salvation of all. As the Jews on the whole prove unreceptive to His message,

He gradually enlarges it to include non-Jews. The mission of Jesus was one of reconciliation of all humanity with His Father. Reconciliation must play an important role in our own religion, even with people who may be different from us or who do not think as we do. We are all brothers and sisters, children of a common Father.

Twelfth Sunday of the Year   < A

Theme: There are many times in our lives when by our words or actions we must declare ourselves for or against Christ. In the time of Moses and of Christ, the world was pre-Christian. We now live in a post-Christian world when Christian values are continually challenged. We cannot accept the values of the world.

First Reading (Jer 20:10-13): Jeremiah witnessed the Babylonian conquest and destruction of Jerusalem. His prophecies are filled with great grief, but in today's reading there is an unusual note of optimism. Despite all that is happening, his trust in the Lord is firm.

Responsorial Psalm (Ps 69): Although the psalmist is distressed, he too is confident that God will answer his plea.

Second Reading (Rom 5:12-15): In this important doctrinal reading, Paul compares Christ and Adam. He concludes that through one man sin entered the world and affects us all, so through one man God's grace was restored to all.

Third Reading (Mt 10:26-33): The theme of today's liturgy is stated clearly: "Do not let men intimidate you." This is to be observed even to the extent of losing one's life for the Gospel. Our ultimate confidence is in God, who is concerned even with the death of a single sparrow.

Thought for the Day: How great a role does human respect play in our lives? So many are afraid to live Christian lives because of the opinion of others. We must be in the world but not of it. When values clash, our Christian principles must decide our course of action. If we disown Christ by our deeds, He has promised to disown us.

Thirteenth Sunday of the Year   < A

Theme: God's messengers were not always the most popular of men because they challenged the values and consciences of those who heard their preaching. Yet God expects us to receive them and promises a reward when we do this.

First Reading (2 Kgs 4:8-11, 14-16): There was a woman in Shunem who made welcome the prophet Elisha. As a reward God sent her a son. A later reading tells how this son died and was brought back to life by Elisha. The Gospel lesson is clear: Anyone who welcomes a prophet will receive a prophet's reward.

Responsorial Psalm (Ps 89): A hymn of praise and thankfulness to God for His own faithfulness.

Second Reading (Rom 6:3-4, 8-11): In baptism each of us died to sin and was reborn in Christ. For Paul baptism is no mere symbol but a triumph of faith by which the Christian is expected to be free from sin and to live a life of faith.

Third Reading (Mt 10:37-42): The Gospels record a number of major sermons of Christ: the Sermon on the Mount, the Last Supper sermon and this one, in which He commissions His apostles and gives them their missionary charge. Today's passage concludes this sermon. While addressed to the apostles, there is a message for all of us: Whoever receives God's teachers and shows the slightest kindness will be rewarded.

Thought for the Day: Today's Gospel records one of the great paradoxes of Christianity. The way to Christ is by suffering and self-denial. It is by losing our life that we find it. This teaching is contrary to all of the world's values and goes to the very heart of the Christian message. Our relationships with others must be ones of giving and not taking.

Fourteenth Sunday of the Year   < A

Theme: The lesson of today's liturgy is one of humility. Christ himself is portrayed by the prophet as meek and humble. His own Gospel teaching contains the same message for His followers.

First Reading (Zec 9:9-10): Outside of Isaiah, this is one of

34

the most important prophecies of the Old Testament. Zechariah describes the Messiah as a king who enters His city of Jerusalem on the colt of an ass, proclaiming a gospel of peace.

Responsorial Psalm (Ps 145): A hymn of praise to the Lord which depicts Him as meek, gentle and full of kindness.

Second Reading (Rom 8:9, 11-13): Our whole spiritual life flows from the Holy Spirit, uniting us through our baptism in a special way to Christ. If we live in the Spirit we can be sure of eternal life.

Third Reading (Mt 11:25-30): Although at first glance the obvious message of this Gospel is Christ's gentleness and humility, this is a much more important reading. Nowhere else outside of St. John's Gospel is the closeness of Jesus and the Father so clearly stated. It is only the Father and Son who thoroughly know each other. This identification is of great theological importance.

Thought for the Day: Jesus Christ was both God and man, a teaching today's liturgy develops for us. While we can look on Jesus as our brother, we cannot become so buddy-buddy as to forget that He is also our God, worthy of our adoration. This is important to remember today when some inventive liturgies forget the great majesty of God.

Fifteenth Sunday of the Year   < A

Theme: The Word of God is the true food and the nourishment necessary for eternal life. That Word was spoken by God in the person of Jesus Christ. It is our choice how we receive that Word, and the fruit each of us bears depends on our reply.

First Reading (Is 55:10-11): Isaiah likens God's Word to the rain that falls and gives us nourishment. God does not speak in vain but accomplishes what He wills by His Word.

Responsorial Psalm (Ps 65): Again, the psalmist sees God as a master farmer responsible for a rich harvest.

Second Reading (Rom 8:18-23): Paul envisions all creation being redeemed by the Spirit of God. He looks forward to his own resurrection as fully completing life.

Third Reading (Mt 13:1-23): At first glance the parable of the sower seems obvious and we may wonder why Christ must explain it privately to His apostles. Redemption involves the virtues of hope and faith, for no man can be sure of it. Therefore, we cannot approach our redemption with logic. Quoting Isaiah, Our Lord indicates many of His hearers are not ready to make this commitment to faith.

Thought for the Day: Christ's parable is a warning to all of us. Through baptism God plants His Word in our soul, but it is up to each one of us to nourish it and make it grow so that it will bear the fruit God intends, namely our redemption and salvation.

Sixteenth Sunday of the Year < A

Theme: Once again the Church speaks to us about the mystery of salvation, saying that God offers it to all, staying His wrath as long as He can. He is always ready to receive our repentance.

First Reading (Wis 12:13, 16-19): The twelfth chapter of the Book of Wisdom concerns the Canaanites, who for many years blocked the entrance of the Israelites into the Promised Land. The author explains that God moved patiently in order to give the Canaanites time to repent and accept Him.

Responsorial Psalm (Ps 86): The Lord forgives all who call upon Him.

Second Reading (Rom 8:26-27): The Spirit pleads to God for us in a way we could never put into words. It is because of the Spirit of Christ dwelling within us that we can call God "Father."

Third Reading (Mt 13:24-43): The long form of the Gospel today contains three parables: the wheat and the cockle, the mustard seed, and the yeast as leaven. What Christ is doing is presenting three different ways of looking at the kingdom of God. The first explains the presence of good and bad in the world, the second shows how God's kingdom grows from a small beginning, and the third demonstrates the tremendous power of grace.

Thought for the Day: There is a personal meaning for each of us in the parable of the wheat and the cockle. Although in its general application it applies to the world, it is also a warning that we must root out of our own hearts those things that would separate us from God. In the spirit of the first reading God withholds His judgment, giving us time to repent, but the day of reckoning must finally come.

Seventeenth Sunday of the Year   <   A

Theme: True wisdom is in knowing what is important in life, then having the courage to follow those insights.

First Reading (1 Kgs 3:5, 7-12): This story of the young Solomon choosing wisdom above any gift God could shower upon him should cause us to ponder on what wisdom really is. Solomon gives us the answer: to distinguish right from wrong. This is important because our salvation depends upon it.

Responsorial Psalm (Ps 119): To keep the commandments of God is true wisdom, more precious than all the gold of the world.

Second Reading (Rom 8:28-30): To those who love God all things work together for good. Loving God means that we respond to Him in faith and hope and that we keep His commandments.

Third Reading (Mt 13:44-52): Our Lord's sermon on the kingdom of heaven which was given in parables concludes with today's reading. The buried treasure and the pearl are symbols of the worth of salvation. No cost is too great to obtain them once we know their value.

Thought for the Day: We must keep in mind the difference between wisdom and knowledge because they are sometimes confused. A man may know all the fine points of philosophy and every nuance of theology, but this knowledge does not mean that he is a person of faith. Wisdom can belong to the simplest of men. All he needs to know is the difference between right and wrong and follow that knowledge.

Eighteenth Sunday of the Year   <   A

Theme: God cares for His people. Under the Old Law, He kept them from starvation on their return from exile. In the new covenant, He gives us himself as a food not of this world.

First Reading (Is 55:1-3): Isaiah refers to God's physical care of His creation. Although his language is in material terms, he refers to a food that is spiritual: the Word of God.

Responsorial Psalm (Ps 145): The Lord loves His people and takes care of them.

Second Reading (Rom 8:35, 37-39): Nothing should separate us from the love of God. If anything comes between us and God, it must be judged worthless. This text is a practical rule for daily living. How are we to know what the love of God is? It is that which Christ showed us by the example of His own life.

Third Reading (Mt 14:13-21): Jesus goes away to be alone with His grief at the death of John the Baptist, but the crowds follow Him, expecting to see more wonders. Ostensibly, he feeds them out of pity at their hunger. Actually, he is preparing them by this miracle for the doctrine of the Eucharist which He will shortly reveal.

Thought for the Day: Not on bread alone does man live but on the Word that comes from God. This Word finds its fullest expression in Jesus Christ. He is our heavenly and eternal food. Jesus gives the manna of the New Covenant, which is himself.

Nineteenth Sunday of the Year < A

Theme: God reveals himself in the elements of nature, but His presence is not always in sound and fury, in great natural phenomena. Sometimes He is a whisper barely heard and we must be ready and quick to catch His message.

First Reading (1 Kgs 19:9, 11-13): Scripture gives a mystical quality to mountains. Here man has his most intimate contacts with God. The high places are closely related to great moments in the lives of Moses, Elijah and Christ. In lofty solitude man communes with God. In this reading Elijah, high on Mount Horeb, awaits the coming of God and finds Him in a gentle breath of wind.

Responsorial Psalm (Ps 85): Peace, God's greatest blessing, is the fruit of justice.

Second Reading (Rom 9:1-5): This is one of the few times that Paul lets his deep-seated feelings for his people reveal themselves. His love for them is so great that he could accept condemnation for himself if that would make them accept the Messiah.

Third Reading (Mt 14:22-23): Although this reading shows the power of Christ over the elements of nature, its true message is the necessity of faith. Peter typically acts boldly and confidently, but Christ teaches him that he is still not wholly rid of self. There is much more to faith than admitting that Jesus is the Son of God.

Thought for the Day: We must truly withdraw from the world to find God. Oh, there are evidences of Him in a sunset, a mighty wind, a great storm; but His deepest secrets are revealed to us in silence. How still we must be, how acute our senses, to hear a breath!

Twentieth Sunday of the Year   < A

Theme: Christ came to give eternal life to all peoples of all nations.

First Reading (Is 56:1, 6-7): This reading is unusual in Old Testament literature because Isaiah speaks of the salvation of non-Jews. The Jews looked upon themselves as the sole Chosen People of God, and when a convert was made to Judaism, such as Achior in the Book of Judith, it was unusual enough that it was commented upon in Scripture. This prophecy reveals a God of the nations and not just the God of the Jews.

Responsorial Psalm (Ps 67): An invitation to all nations to praise the one, true God.

Second Reading (Rom 11:13-15, 29-32): Paul gives himself the name of Apostle to the Gentiles. Yet he reminds his Gentile hearers that they owe their faith to the infidelity of the Jews. He hopes that through other nations Israel will one day recognize Christ.

Third Reading (Mt 15:21-28): The Canaanites were despised by the Jews. In fact the Promised Land was wrested from its Canaanite inhabitants. Jesus tells the Canaanite woman His teaching is meant for the Jews, but her great faith moves Jesus, foreshadowing the day when His mission will be directed beyond the Jews.

Thought for the Day: Today's readings are rich in theological thought and could take many pages to expound. Just as the messiahship of Jesus is recognized by a pagan woman when it has been rejected by the leaders of His own people, so are all people given the opportunity to find salvation in Christ. But how will they know Him unless we tell them? Each of us has a role in making Christ known. This is the mission given us in baptism.

Twenty-first Sunday of the Year   < A

Theme: God entrusts His mission to us. In the Old Testament He raised up great prophets. In the New Testament He has ordered His mission under Peter, the apostles and their successors.

First Reading (Is 22:15, 19-23): At God's command the prophet Isaiah was advocating a policy of neutrality between Egypt and Assyria. The palace steward, Shebna, opposed him. As a result, God caused Shebna to be deposed and raised up Eliakim, in whom the Church sees a prototype for Peter.

Responsorial Psalm (Ps 138): A hymn of thanksgiving for God's loving concern and a prayer that it will remain constant.

Second Reading (Rom 11:33-36): This is Paul's famous prayer of praise for God's wisdom. God directs all things to accomplish the end He has determined.

Third Reading (Mt 16:13-20): This is one of the most important readings for the Church and one over which many have stumbled in the past. In it Peter is confirmed by Jesus as head of His Church. Jesus gives him the keys of the kingdom of heaven. It is this power that is passed down through Peter to his successors and makes the pope infallible and gives us the surety that our sins are forgiven in confession. Christ is slowly building the structures of His Church, but He is not yet ready to have himself revealed openly.

Thought for the Day: In these days, when the authority of the pope is under attack from even within the Church, this liturgy reminds us that through the pope we are linked to Peter and through Peter to Christ. Later Christ promises to be with His Church for all days, and He is visibly with us through the pope, the servant of the servants of God.

Twenty-second Sunday of the Year   < A

Theme: Suffering is one of life's mysteries. It is hard to reconcile human pain with a good and loving God. Yet the lives of the greatest saints were marked by tremendous external and internal suffering. Since God can will no evil, mankind's view of suffering must be in error.

First Reading (Jer 20:7-9): In this very personal passage, the prophet Jeremiah tells of his own suffering brought about by doing the work of God. Men mock and deride him for his message and this hurts. Even his desire to spread the Word of God gives him pain.

Responsorial Psalm (Ps 63): Jeremiah's longing finds an echo in this psalm. Yet this same longing gives us a great hymn of faith.

Second Reading (Rom 12:1-2): Paul warns the Romans not to allow themselves to be influenced by the paganism in which they live but to offer their lives to God, seeking only to do His will. It is a message very applicable to our own pagan times.

Third Reading (Mt 16:21-27): Jesus has finished His description of the kingdom of heaven and now turns His attention to the suffering and death that lie ahead. His apostles, still thinking in terms of an earthly kingdom, rebel at the thought that Jesus will have to suffer and die. Jesus gives us the key to the acceptance of suffering: "You are not judging by God's standards but by man's." Then He indicates all of us must imitate Him.

Thought for the Day: Some spiritual writers have likened suffering to the shadow that falls on the earth when a cloud blocks the sun. It is the lack of a good. Certainly, Christ's view of suffering is not that of mankind, which seeks through drugs to escape the least suffering. Jesus saw it as the only way to His Father.

Twenty-third Sunday of the Year   < A

Theme: Today's liturgy is concerned with fraternal correction. Paul best sums it up in his statement of the Golden Rule: "You shall love your neighbor as yourself."

First Reading (Ez 33:7-9): Ezekiel is charged by God to be a guardian of the people's morals and is told that if he fails to rebuke evil, he shares in its guilt. If his warning goes unheeded, then he has done all God expects of him.

Responsorial Psalm (Ps 95): The psalmist exhorts us not to close our hearts to the voice of God which speaks to us through our consciences.

Second Reading (Rom 13:8-10): Paul sums up the social and negative commandments of the Old Law into the single social commandment of Christ: "You shall love your neighbor as yourself." This is the fulfillment of God's law.

Third Reading (Mt 18:15-20): The Gospel today has a number of viewpoints. The first is in keeping with the theme of the liturgy that we should correct the fault of a brother. Jesus also reminds His apostles of the power of the keys which He has previously given, to bind or release men from their sins. Finally, He promises that God will hear group prayer and that where several are gathered to pray in His name, He will be among them in His spirit.

Thought for the Day: We live in a very permissive society in which we are expected to allow everyone to do his own thing. Even parents are instructed not to correct or rebuke their children lest they give them some psychological inhibitions. All of this is of course nonsense. If we truly love our neighbors, the greatest good we can want for them is their salvation. Therefore, at times it may be necessary to remind them that some action is separating them from God. It is not popular at times to rebuke even kindly, but love may demand that we do this.

Twenty-fourth Sunday of the Year   < A

Theme: The Golden Rule.

First Reading (Sir 27:30 — 28:7): The nomadic law which the ancestors of Israel followed was one of vengeance — an eye for an eye, a tooth for a tooth. But God's revelation to His Chosen People was one of forgiveness and love. Sirach bids us to remember our own end. If we have not forgiven, we will not be forgiven.

Responsorial Psalm (Ps 103): It is God who gives forgiveness, not according to our sins, but from His love, freely given.

Second Reading (Rom 14:7-9): "Both in life and death we are the Lord's," Paul reminds us. He has been speaking of the fact that we should not pass judgment on one another. It is not a question of who is right or wrong if you and the other person are both trying to please God. That in the end is what really counts.

Third Reading (Mt 18:21-35): The answer of Jesus to Peter's question about the frequency of forgiveness places no limit on the mercy we are expected to show. The parable clearly shows that mercy is without limit, particularly since God forgives our own great debts.

Thought for the Day: Religion is too often reduced to mere platitudes, and the Golden Rule can become one unless it is an activating force in our lives. It is not what we say but what we do that counts. How many Catholic families are divided by some bitterness! The reason is that our love for God is not truly real. If we do love God, we will love others. If we do not actively love others, we do not really love God.

Twenty-fifth Sunday of the Year   < A

Theme: God's ways are not our ways.

First Reading (Is 55:6-9): While the prophet places his confidence in God, who is always near us, nevertheless we must recognize that we think and understand with finite minds and can never therefore fully comprehend God or even His manner of acting.

Responsorial Psalm (Ps 145): God is near to all who call upon Him. This concern of God for us is a great mystery. We do not understand how Unsearchable Greatness deigns to deal with a frail human.

Second Reading (Phil 1:20-24, 27): Paul rejects the values of the world. For him life is in dying and he would prefer to die. Yet he chooses to be alive so that he can strengthen the Church he has founded at Philippi. It is the greatest sacrifice he can make for his beloved converts.

Third Reading (Mt 20:1-16): The traditional explanation of today's parable is that the vineyard owner represents God selecting the Gentiles at a late hour to share in His kingdom. But it also tells us something about God's grace and values. Many will be saved at the last moment, but on this we cannot presume.

Thought for the Day: The thought must occur to us at one time or another that it does not seem just that a person who ignores and sins against God through most of his life should be saved and taken to heaven at the moment of death, while most of us have to live a lifetime of struggling to do the will of God. The answer to this problem is in the Gospel today. The reward of the kingdom is His gift. His manner of judging is far different from that of man. Although God made a covenant with Israel, He was prepared to broaden it to all men late in time. We do not understand His reasons, but we know by faith that they are valid.

Twenty-sixth Sunday of the Year < A

Theme: God's standards for judging are different than ours. No one because of position can presume salvation. Belief in God is far different than knowing about Him.

First Reading (Ez 18:25-28): In Babylonia, Ezekiel speaks to the captured Israelites. He is answering their complaints about their captivity. Although they are being punished for sins of their fathers, they themselves can find salvation because God is there with them in Babylonia.

Responsorial Psalm (Ps 25): A plea for deliverance which asks God not to remember past sins.

Second Reading (Phil 2:1-11): This reading contains one of the most beautiful passages in Paul's writings. Paul is insisting on unity among his Christians. Only through this unity can they become more like Christ and share His life. He then goes on to describe the sacrifice of Christ, which has exalted Him above all.

Third Reading (Mt 21:28-32): Jesus tells the people of Jerusalem that they have no special claim on His kingdom. Obedience to the will of God is the real test. Many on whom the Jews looked down accept the word of Christ, while those who are supposed to be religious reject it. For this reason salvation is passing them by and sinners are being accepted into the kingdom.

Thought for the Day: It is easy to give obedience in words, but true obedience is proved in the manner of the second son through action. God has given Christ to be our model. Our success as a Christian depends upon how well we reproduce Christ in our own lives and not in our intentions or even the prayers we say.

Twenty-seventh Sunday of the Year   < A

Theme: The liturgy likens the people of God to a vineyard in which God expects to produce good fruit; if it does not, then it will be destroyed.

First Reading (Is 5:1-7): God has made a covenant with the people of Israel and has done everything possible for them, even to sending them prophets to remind them of their errors. But God's wrath at the failures of Israel will not be put aside forever. The day of reckoning is at hand when God's mercy will no longer be shown.

Responsorial Psalm (Ps 80): The vineyard analogy is carried forward by the psalmist, who asks God to make the vineyard of Israel prosper.

Second Reading (Phil 4:6-9): Paul continues his advice to his converts at Philippi. God's own peace and harmony should be their model if they are to have faith and love. When life is thus lived, the Philippians will find the peace which comes only from God.

Third Reading (Mt 21:33-43): God's patience has its limits. Isaiah states this in the first reading, and now the Gospel repeats the thought. Jesus applies the parable to himself, likening himself to a cornerstone rejected by builders. Because of this rejection the people of Israel have run out of time. God's vineyard will be put in the hands of people from other nations.

Thought for the Day: How closely do I adhere to the Word of God? Do I produce good fruit or bad? Do I fully accept and practice the teachings of Christ, or can I be accused of rejecting the cornerstone?

Twenty-eighth Sunday of the Year   < A

Theme: While the main thrust of today's liturgy is historical, the promise of a Messiah and the invitation of Jews to be members of His kingdom, we are reminded of the mercy of God, which makes that kingdom available to each one of us.

First Reading (Is 25:6-10): Isaiah returns to a familiar Old Testament theme couched in terms of the mysticism of mountains. This time the mountain refers to Jerusalem, restored after its devastation. It is a symbol of the messianic age. God will again visit His people, and His salvation offer will never end.

Responsorial Psalm (Ps 23): This song of David, which pictures God as a shepherd, is a longtime favorite of Catholics and Protestants.

Second Reading (Phil 4:12-14, 19-20): Paul had a special relationship with the community of Philippi. It was the only one from which he ever accepted financial assistance. He instructs his converts to rely on God and to judge their actions according to God's standards. An important point is that he says the Philippians should follow his example and not just his words.

Third Reading (Mt 22:1-14): Still speaking in parables, Jesus tells the Jews that by weak excuses they are rejecting the Messiah and stand in danger of losing the kingdom of heaven entirely. Even those who understand His teachings must be prepared to put on the wedding garment of faith or they too will be rejected.

Thought for the Day: Everyone is free to reject God's invitation to share in His divine life. If we accept, we must fulfill the necessary condition, which for us is fidelity to His Church and its teachings.

Twenty-ninth Sunday of the Year   < A

Theme: God often uses seemingly unlikely instruments to have His will accomplished, which is that all must recognize Him as the one and only true God.

First Reading (Is 45:1, 4-6): It might be wondered how the Persian king Cyprus can be called the anointed of the Lord, a term usually reserved for the kings and prophets of Israel. It was Cyrus, who in his conquest of Babylon, freed the Israelites from captivity, thus becoming an instrument of God in the history of His people, enabling them to worship freely again.

Responsorial Psalm (Ps 96): A hymn stating that God is above all kings and alone worthy of the praise of all.

Second Reading (1 Thes 1:1-5): With the end of the liturgical year approaching, the Church wants us to remember the Second Coming of Christ and hence uses this letter of St. Paul, which has the Second Coming as its theme. In this introduction Paul praises his converts for their faith and love and particularly their firmness in their hope in Jesus Christ.

Third Reading (Mt 22:15-21): While the classical lesson in this reading is the separation of church and state and the rendering of the debts due to each, even Caesar, like Cyrus, is going to play a role in the spread of God's kingdom. The Pax Romana will enable the Gospel to spread through most of the civilized world.

Thought for the Day: The work of God must be carried on like that of Paul: in the Holy Spirit and out of complete conviction. God uses human instruments like ourselves to spread His kingdom, but we must cooperate out of our belief. We are reminded today that we must give to God what is God's, which includes His people and His world. Our actions must be directed by our faith.

Thirtieth Sunday of the Year < A

Theme: The theme of the liturgy today is important because it is the summary of the New Law: love of God and love of neighbor.

First Reading (Ex 22:20-26): The first reading is taken from the long Book of the Covenant, the law dictated to Moses by God. In this passage God commands that he will not brook injustice from His people, neither to strangers, nor to the weak or helpless. God's wrath will punish transgressors.

Responsorial Psalm (Ps 18): A hymn of praise to God for His protection.

Second Reading (1 Thes 1:5-10): Paul praises the Church in Thessalonica for the example it gives to the rest of Greece, despite the persecution and trials that beset it.

Third Reading (Mt 22:34-40): Let us not be distracted today by the trap set by Jewish leaders for Jesus, because His answer is too important to concern ourselves with its context. Jesus gives a reply that summarizes the New Law in two commandments, which summarize all the prescripts of the Old Covenant.

47

It is not the answer His questioners expected, but it is a way of life for each one of us.

Thought for the Day: There are some today who preach that our love for God is expressed in our love of neighbor. While this is true, there is a danger in the statement that it focuses too great attention on our neighbor to the exclusion of God. The command of Christ was in two parts: love of God and love of neighbor. If we do not practice the first part in all that it implies, then our love of neighbor is mere humanism, which is a great error of our times.

Thirty-first Sunday of the Year   < A

Theme: Those who have the responsibility of teaching others must themselves observe the things they teach. We must practice what we preach.

First Reading (Mal 1:14 — 2:2, 8-10): In this passage, Malachi is comparing the priesthood of earlier days with that of his own time and finds it wanting. Instead of guiding, the priests themselves go astray and lead others astray. The Church applies these thoughts to each one of us.

Responsorial Psalm (Ps 131): Trust God like a child trusts its mother.

Second Reading (1 Thes 2:7-9, 13). Evidently someone at Thessalonica has been attempting to undermine Paul by accusing him of base motives. He writes a defense of his conduct, saying that his preaching was pure and disinterested.

Third Reading (Mt 23:1-12): In speaking to his disciples about their attitude toward the scribes and Pharisees, Jesus makes an important distinction. They must not reject the authority of the scribes and Pharisees who teach with the authority of Moses, but neither should they imitate the hypocrisy of their lives. They do not practice what they preach. Jesus condemns the false adulation given these teachers. Rabbi literally means "my great one." Hence verse 11 becomes a pun. Jesus reminds them that he is their teacher.

Thought for the Day: Example is the best teacher. Malachi speaks of bad example. Paul speaks of his own example. Jesus speaks of bad example. Our lives are the best preaching we do.

Thirty-second Sunday of the Year   < A

Theme: As we approach the end of the liturgical year, the liturgy turns to Christ's Second Coming. Today we are told to keep ourselves ready.

First Reading (Wis 6:12-16): The aim of the writer of the Book of Wisdom is to encourage his readers to seek wisdom and so gain eternal life. In this reading we are told that wisdom is found by those who seek it.

Responsorial Psalm (Ps 63): True wisdom is a desire for God.

Second Reading (1 Thes 4:13-18): The Christians at Thessalonica are concerned about what happens to those who die before the Second Coming. Paul assures them that the dead will be raised, and together with the living faithful will enjoy union with Christ. Paul's teaching is not one to cause anxiety but consolation.

Third Reading (Mt 25:1-13): The parable of the ten bridesmaids is a lesson on preparedness for the coming of Christ. It will happen unexpectedly, perhaps even in the reaches of the night. The cry of the girls outside the locked door reminds us of Our Lord's warning, "None of those who cry out, 'Lord, Lord,' will enter the kingdom of my Father in heaven" (Mt 7:21).

Thought for the Day: Christ will not make an appointment with us. The only way of being sure to be ready when He comes is by daily Christian living. Our life must revolve around Jesus so that we are prepared to meet Him at any time.

Thirty-third Sunday of the Year   < A

Theme: Although the readings today are diverse, they do point out that each must use the talents given by God to perfect his or her state in life.

First Reading (Prv 31:10-13, 19-20, 30-31): This is a summary from the end of the Book of Proverbs on what constitutes a perfect wife. This reading may annoy members of the women's liberation movement. It must be understood in the context of its time, when a woman's expected role was that of a wife who fulfills the duties of her home and still has time to show charity to the needy.

Responsorial Psalm (Ps 128): Respect for God is the keystone of a happy home.

Second Reading (1 Thes 5:1-6): St. Paul frequently repeats the theme that we should be ready for the coming of Christ and not be like the rest of the world, which is caught up in its own cares.

Third Reading (Mt 25:14-30): This parable of the talents is not an easy parable to understand. It refers to God's judgment and His accounting of the personal gifts He has bestowed on us. It also refers to the Jews who have rejected the great gift offered through Christ. The basic meaning is that each of us must account for his or her stewardship.

Thought for the Day: A person who thinks only of himself or herself will fail God. A good wife is a success because she is also concerned with charity outside her home. The successful steward is willing to take a chance to please his master. God gives all of us certain talents and expects us to use them. We might consider today what account we would render if we were suddenly called to judgment.

Feast of Christ the King
(Last Sunday of the Year)   < A

Theme: Jesus Christ is king of heaven and earth and all belong to His kingdom.

First Reading (Ez 34:11-12, 15-17): Christ must have had this passage of Ezekiel in mind when He called himself the Good Shepherd. God, through Christ, will seek out all men, offering His aid and salvation. Some will refuse His rule and will have to be separated from the flock.

Responsorial Psalm (Ps 23): This is a favorite psalm of all Christians. With the Lord as our shepherd we need have no worry or concerns. He will care for all of our needs and keep us with himself always.

Second Reading (1 Cor 15:20-26, 28): If mankind died through Adam, all men have been restored to God's life through Christ. He is our guardian, our shepherd, our king, to whom all of us must be subject. Christ will destroy death and offer everlasting life to all so that God may be all in all.

Third Reading (Mt 25:31-46): Jesus is quickly approaching His death, but before Matthew turns to the Passion account he recalls Christ's description of himself as king, who has come in judgment on the nations. Christ has already given His commandment of love of neighbor, and His final judgment is on how well we have kept this. The examination described here is not legalistic but on our social relationships.

Thought for the Day: It is easy to say that Christ is king, but do we proclaim this by our deeds? Do our lives show that we recognize His kingship? This is the last Sunday of the liturgical year, and what the Church is saying to us today takes on exceptional importance. Unless we have turned our lives over to Christ and are living His teachings, we are in effect rejecting His kingship and preparing the day of our condemnation.

Year B

Nativity Cycle

First Sunday of Advent   < B

Theme: "Be on guard" is the warning of the liturgy today. The Advent theme is the Second Coming of Christ. We do not know when this will happen, but we must always be ready. As we prepare to celebrate the First Coming, our watch is more than historical.

First Reading (Is 63:16-17, 19; 64:1, 3-8): Isaiah is the great prophet of the First Coming. One can almost feel the agony of his expectation as he exclaims, "Oh, that you would rend the heavens and come down." He sees God as a father in whose hands we are like clay in the hands of the potter.

Responsorial Psalm (Ps 80): A plea to God for salvation.

Second Reading (1 Cor 1:3-9): Paul reminds his converts in Corinth that they must be ready for the coming of Christ. He views this as the day when the Lord will be revealed as He is. The Greeks called this the *parousia*, the coming presence of Christ among us.

Third Reading (Mk 13:33-37): The message of Mark is very clear: "Be constantly on the watch!" The apostles had just asked the Lord when the end of the world would occur. Although He gives some signs, the heart of His message is in today's Gospel in that we must be watchful. In actuality the Lord is never really absent, but His Second Coming will have a dramatic effect on our lives.

Thought for the Day: While we must be watchful for the coming of the Lord, He does not expect us to sit idly by in expectation. This period of waiting is a period of work when we gather the harvest. It should be a period of intense missionary activity so that all may know and love the Lord at His coming.

Second Sunday of Advent   < B

Theme: Preparation for the coming of Christ moves forward. The liturgy today gives us the example of John the Baptist, who was attempting to prepare the world for Jesus.

First Reading (Is 40:1-5, 9-11): There is much biblical symbolism in this reading from Isaiah. Not only do the words of the prophet foreshadow John the Bapist, but Isaiah foretells the redemption of Jerusalem by a Savior who will be a good shepherd, one of great power yet with remarkable tenderness.

Responsorial Psalm (Ps 85): The psalmist sees salvation coming to us as kindness, truth, justice and peace.

Second Reading (2 Pt 3:8-14): Peter reminds us that, while the time of waiting for the Lord may seem long to us, time is of no consequence to God. With Him a thousand years is but a day. Instead, we should use the time to prepare ourselves for our own personal meeting with the Lord.

Third Reading (Mk 1:1-8): Mark chooses John's preaching as the scene with which to open his Gospel and set the stage for his presentation of Christ. He considers John's testimony to be of great importance because John's mission is to prepare the way for Christ, who will bring mankind the great gift of the Spirit.

Thought for the Day: There are two preparations we must make as Christians. The first is personal preparation of ourselves to meet the Lord. Advent is a time to focus in on this need. We must also prepare the world for the Lord. There is great uncertainty in the world today, and the great service Christians can make is to help their nonbelieving neighbors to be ready to receive Christ into their own hearts.

Third Sunday of Advent < B

Theme: In the Entrance Prayer, Paul sets the theme of joyous expectation when he exclaims: "Rejoice in the Lord always! I say it again, rejoice! The Lord is near" (Phil 4:4).

First Reading (Is 61:1-2, 10-11): This is an important reading from Isaiah because St. Luke begins his account of the public life of Jesus by having Christ quote this prophecy to prove the authenticity of His mission. While the prophet is undoubtedly speaking of himself, his spirit is a messianic spirit that foreshadows Christ.

Responsorial Psalm (Lk 1:46-50, 53-54): In place of the usual psalm, verses are taken from Our Lady's canticle, The Magnificat, to carry forward the spirit of the first reading.

Second Reading (1 Thes 5:16-24): The end of Paul's letter is both a greeting and a prayer. Paul reminds his converts to pray always that God will make us perfect in holiness so that we will be ready to greet His Son.

Third Reading (Jn 1:6-8, 19-28): John follows up the prologue to his Gospel with the testimony of John the Baptist that his role is to prepare the way for Christ. He tells all that he is not the Messiah but that the one they are looking for is now among them.

Thought for the Day: The Church is moving ever closer to the celebration of the birthday of our Savior. During these Sundays of Advent we have been presented with the signs from Scripture — the prophecies of Isaiah, the testimony of Mary, the preaching of John the Baptist. Now looking forward to that day we rejoice that the hour of our redemption is at hand in the coming of our Messiah.

Fourth Sunday of Advent < B

Theme: The kingdom of God is at hand. In Christ, David's kingdom is made secure for all time. As Paul tells us, the mystery hidden through the ages is now made known to all men for all time through Jesus Christ.

First Reading (2 Sm 7:1-5, 8-11, 16): There is a contrast in this prophecy from Samuel. David promises to build a house for

God while God, in turn, promises a royal house for David, from whose lineage Christ will come.

Responsorial Psalm (Ps 89): The psalmist reflects on the promise made to David — the confirmation of his posterity built on the firm rock of a covenant.

Second Reading (Rom 16:25-27): Paul tells the Romans that the Gospel which he has preached to them reveals God's great mystery, Jesus Christ, whose coming was prepared for ages. That which was veiled in prophecy is now made plain for all times through Christ.

Third Reading (Mk 1:26-38): As a direct preparation for Christmas, the liturgy recounts the Annunciation account. Mary is to become the temple of God's Son, but before that can happen her consent must be given. Although there is directness in this Gospel, there is also great mystery, which troubles Mary because she wishes to preserve her virginity. When she is assured that this will be possible, she acknowledges her dependence on God and gives her consent.

Thought for the Day: Although the humanity of Christ can be known to us because of our own experience, His divinity will always remain a mystery. We must always remember that Christ is both God and man. We can approach Him as our brother but must also stand in awe of Him as our Creator.

Christmas: See Year A, pages 4-6.

Holy Family (Sunday in Octave of Christmas): See Year A, page 6.

Mary, Mother of God (Jan. 1): See Year A, page 7.

Epiphany (Sunday between Jan. 2-8): See Year A, page 8.

Baptism of the Lord (First Sunday of the Year, Sunday after Epiphany): See Year A, page 9.

Paschal Cycle

First Sunday of Lent   < B

Theme: The presence of evil, and baptism and penance are three Lenten considerations, and all appear in this liturgy. In Noah's story there is a foreshadowing of salvation and the Resurrection.

First Reading (Gn 9:8-15): Although the people sin and must be punished, God renews through Noah His covenant with man, confirming it in that wonder of nature, a rainbow.

Responsorial Psalm (Ps 25): A petition asking God to teach the way of righteousness so that sin can be avoided.

Second Reading (1 Pt 3:18-22): Peter compares baptism to the salvation of Noah, noting the difference that in Noah's day all but eight perished, but now all can be reborn through Christ.

Third Reading (Mk 1:12-15): Mark's Gospel is concerned with Christ preaching His message in the face of the hostility of Satan. For many years Satan had seemed to have gained the rule of the world. Now he meets defeat in the person of Christ, who then goes forth to preach the Good News that will end Satan's reign forever.

Thought for the Day: The most important words in English are usually very simple. Take the word "water" for example. Water covers three-fourths of our globe. It is an absolute necessity for the continuation of vegetable and animal life. Water too is a necessity for eternal life, for baptism is our gateway to heaven. Baptism opens a whole new relationship between humanity and God. Jesus began His public life by submitting to the baptism of John. Next He went into the Lent of the desert, where for forty days He did penance. Only then did He begin His preaching. Our Lent is a time to revivify our baptismal promise and to prepare ourselves by penance.

Second Sunday of Lent   < B

Theme: There is much theological significance in the readings today. The interaction between the Father and Son has an effect on all of us.

First Reading (Gn 22:1-2, 9-13, 15-18): In the hindsight of the New Covenant, we see the master plan of God developing through the Old. The sacrifice of Abraham, so difficult to understand, typifies the sacrifice of the Father which was carried through to completion. The parallel between Abraham and Isaac and the Father and Jesus is too strong to be coincidental.

Responsorial Psalm (Ps 116): Again the note of sacrifice is sounded.

Second Reading (Rom 8:31-34): Paul reflects on God's great love for us and the demands we can make on God. He reasons that God, who so loved us that He delivered His own Son to death, will out of that love give us that which we need.

Third Reading (Mk 9:2-10): God ordinarily makes His presence felt away from distractions. On a high mountain He spoke to Moses and in lonely places to Elijah. Now on another mountain these great prophets appear as the Father gives His blessing to the Son. Jesus uses the incident to prepare his beloved apostles for His resurrection. There are strong parallels here with the Old Testament.

Thought for the Day: At the Transfiguration God told man to listen to His Son. Almost immediately Jesus speaks of His passion and death. The Cross is not easy for us to understand since it violates all human instincts, but God is with the just and His promise endures.

Third Sunday of Lent   < B

Theme: The sign of God's covenant with Abraham was in the Ten Commandments given to Moses, and in the New Covenant it is the cross and resurrection of Christ.

First Reading (Ex 20:1-17): The Ten Commandments are the laws given by God for the conduct of men. They were given to the Israelites when they were three months into their flight from Egypt. While Israel was camped at the foot of Mount Sinai, Moses ascended to the top of the mountain. There in the clouds, surrounded by thunder and lightning, the voice of God delivered the way of life. Israel was never again the same.

Responsorial Psalm (Ps 19): God's glory is seen in His law.

Second Reading (1 Cor 1:22-25): For the Jews, who look for signs, and the Greeks, who seek mental exercises, the cross of Christ answers both. It is a sign of salvation and a contradiction that can never be fully fathomed.

Third Reading (Jn 2:13-25): The heart of today's Gospel is not in the cleansing of the Temple — that is a preparatory act. It is the declaration of Jesus of His own resurrection. This was to be the sign that would confirm His entire life. The pieces of history are falling into place and building to a magnificent, stupendous and incomprehensible climax that can be understood only through faith.

Thought for the Day: Lent is a time for preparation, for checking our obedience to God's law. It all culminates in our identification with and absorption into the mystical life of the risen Christ.

Fourth Sunday of Lent   < B

Theme: The love of God for a sinful humanity is today's theme. Although the Israelites departed from the ways of the Lord and although many prefer darkness to the light of Christ, God's mercy will always be at hand.

First Reading (2 Chr 36:14-17, 19-23): For their infidelity, the Israelites are sent into a seventy-year captivity with Jerusalem and the land of Israel is left desolate. Israel is rescued only by an alien, the Persian king Cyrus.

Responsorial Psalm (Ps 137): A lament of the Babylonian exile.

Second Reading (Eph 2:4-10): Just as Israel became desolate through the exile of its people but was restored, we are saved from the death of sin through Christ. This is God's gift and nothing that we deserve.

Third Reading (Jn 3:14-21): This Gospel proclaims John's great theme: God so loved the world that He gave His only-begotten Son. Salvation comes through faith in this Son. The Israelites in the desert were saved from the bite of fiery serpents by looking up to the bronze serpent of Moses. So we are saved by looking in faith to the Cross.

Thought for the Day: In the verses preceding today's Gospel, Jesus stresses to Nicodemus the necessity of baptism.

Even we who are baptized lose our baptismal integrity through sin and neglect. The Cross stands always as a reminder of our need for penance.

Fifth Sunday of Lent < B

Theme: The moment of the New Covenant is at hand when Christ will deliver himself up as a worthy offering to the Father, a victim of sin, whose sufferings bring salvation.

First Reading (Jer 31:31-34): This is a radical reading. The Old Testament makes frequent reference to the covenant made between God and Israel at the time of Exodus. Now, in a most unusual passage, Jeremiah speaks of a new covenant which is to come. This is a covenant which will take place in our innermost beings when we give ourselves to Christ.

Responsorial Psalm (Ps 51): A plea for forgiveness.

Second Reading (Heb 5:7-9): Jesus was the perfect sacrifice, who through obedience became the salvation offered to all.

Third Reading (Jn 12:20-33): Foreigners come to learn of Jesus, but He is concerned with His own death, which will be a sign to all men. He sees His sacrifice as a glorification of the Father and as a lesson to each of us, who also must die to self if we are to be resurrected.

Thought for the Day: The Christian cannot separate his or her life from that of Christ. We die to sin in baptism and enter a new life but are in constant need of reconciliation (penance), as daily events tend to lead us away from the Master. It is only by death to self that we earn resurrection with Christ.

Passion (Palm) Sunday: See Year A, pages 14-15.

Easter Sunday: See Year A, page 15.

Second Sunday of Easter < B

Theme: Total faith in the risen Christ underlies the readings today. This faith is revealed in deeds and in the response to the Holy Spirit who now works through the Church.

First Reading (Acts 4:32-35): Luke gives an example of

primitive Christianity, in which the unity was so great that the believers even shared possessions, leaving it up to the apostles to distribute according to need.

Responsorial Psalm (Ps 118): The psalm used on Easter Sunday is repeated today to emphasize the importance of our debt to God.

Second Reading (1 Jn 5:1-6): It is easy to say that we believe that Jesus Christ is the Son of God, but true faith shows in love of the Father, in love of His children and in keeping God's commandments. Only when we do all these things do we prove our love of God.

Third Reading (Jn 20:19-31): This is an important Gospel, recounting the establishment of the Sacrament of Penance as the first act of the risen Jesus. Sin is an infinite offense against God for which man alone can never make atonement. But through the merits gained by the redemptive sacrifice of Christ, sin can now be forgiven. Christ waited until this moment to give us penance.

Thought for the Day: Faith is the key to salvation. This fact is totally clear to the apostle John. But faith alone is fruitless unless it is expressed in our lives and our works. Jesus gives us sacramental help and the Holy Spirit gives enlightenment, but each of us must do his or her own part.

Third Sunday of Easter   <   B

Theme: The liturgy is still concerned with the acceptance of the risen Jesus. Peter proves it by a miracle and preaching, while Luke recounts the dramatic post-resurrection appearance when Christ commanded His followers to preach a Gospel of repentance.

First Reading (Acts 3:13-15, 17-19): In the passage immediately preceding this sermon, Peter cures a man crippled since birth. He then begins a sermon of explanation which shows the close connection between sin and healing. He tells the Jews that they crucified Christ through ignorance and summons them to reformation and conversion.

Responsorial Psalm (Ps 4): A song of confidence in the security God gives.

Second Reading (1 Jn 2:1-5): Jesus Christ redeems us from our sins. We are called to live a sinless life, for it is by keeping the commandments that the love of God is made perfect in us.

Third Reading (Lk 24:35-48): Jesus' appearance after His resurrection is startling to the apostles. First He proves that He is no mere vision. Then He instructs His disciples to preach a Gospel of repentance for the forgiveness of sin, not just to Israel but to the whole world.

Thought for the Day: Sin is a reality of our existence. It is the one thing that separates us from God. Christ, through His suffering and conquering of death, has proven His mastery over sin. Jesus offers us this power if we will but live His Gospel.

Fourth Sunday of Easter   < B

Theme: We are not merely creatures of God but children of a heavenly Father. The image of the Good Shepherd tells us of God's concern for us.

First Reading (Acts 4:8-12): Peter's sermon, begun last week, is continued. Jesus is the foundation of the new Church. Through His resurrection He proved His credentials from the Father. It is only through Jesus that salvation comes.

Responsorial Psalm (Ps 118): The stone which the builders rejected has become the cornerstone.

Second Reading (1 Jn 3:1-2): John rejoices in the fact that we are children of God. At this time we know the Father only through faith, but the time will come when we will be able to see God face to face.

Third Reading (Jn 10:11-18): The shepherd is an important biblical figure. David once guarded sheep with his own life and then was appointed to be shepherd of Israel. Now Jesus has become the Good Shepherd of all mankind. In this discourse, Jesus defines the role of a shepherd and then shows how He fulfills it. His gaze goes beyond the sheepfold of Israel, and His hope is that there will be but one flock and one Shepherd for the whole world. That flock will be the Church He founds.

Thought for the Day: The imagery today is one of closeness. There is an intimate relationship between a shepherd and his flock. The relationship is even closer between a father and his children. God is presented to us not as ruler and judge but as a loving person whom we can understand.

Fifth Sunday of Easter   < B

Theme: The test of our Christianity is the degree of our union with Christ, which has its proof in our living of the commandments.

First Reading (Acts 9:26-31): Paul's conversion is not readily accepted by the apostles. They remember his anti-Christianity and persecution of the Church. Barnabas comes to his defense, and his strongest argument is that like the apostles Paul has seen the risen Christ and this has worked such a transformation that Paul now fearlessly defends that which he once opposed, so much so that Jews now seek to kill him.

Responsorial Psalm (Ps 22): This Holy Week psalm is repeated to remind us that God delivers us from evil.

Second Reading (1 Jn 3:18-24): We don't merely talk about love but live it. The proof comes in our belief in Jesus Christ, which compels us to love one another. This is the acid test of our faith.

Third Reading (Jn 15:1-8): Paul will use this teaching of St. John in the development of his own doctrine of the Mystical Body. We can have no true life apart from Christ, and we can bear no worthwhile fruit except through Him.

Thought for the Day: The life of Christ has been given to all baptized, but its growth depends upon our own actions. Only by identifying ourselves with Jesus will we be able to bear the fruits of faith and love. Apart from Him, nothing that we do will have any merit or give any glory to the Father.

Sixth Sunday of Easter   < B

Theme: God is love and our share in God's life comes through our own loving.

First Reading (Acts 10:25-26, 34-35, 44-48): Peter is prepared for his meeting with Cornelius, the Roman centurion, by a vision from God which opens His Church to all peoples. When Peter does meet the Gentile Cornelius, he gives orders that Cor-

nelius and the members of his family are to be baptized.
Responsorial Psalm (Ps 98): Praise to God for the salvation which is offered to all nations.

Second Reading (1 Jn 4:7-10): In this famous passage of John, the apostle gives his simple definition of God, which has never been surpassed: God is love. From this profound truth flows creation and redemption, as well as the whole meaning of life.

Third Reading (Jn 15:9-17): The Church continues with Christ's last sermon to His apostles. Christ is speaking of the importance of love in the Christian vocation and gives as the supreme test the readiness of one to lay down his life for others. Christ is shortly to apply this criterion to His own love by accepting the crucifixion.

Thought for the Day: The liturgy today expresses the deepest theological mystery, which can easily be passed over because it is expressed so simply and in so few words. The expression "God is love" can be meditated upon all of one's days and its full meaning never even approached. St. John in his simplicity saw the depths of the message and passes it on to us so that it may be the guide of our lives.

Seventh Sunday of Easter   < B

Theme: The Church directs our attention to unity with God. This is the prayer of Jesus, the hope of St. John and the reason why Peter wants to restore the integral body of apostles.

First Reading (Acts 1:15-17, 20-26): Christ selected twelve apostles, probably as representative of the twelve tribes of Israel. Peter is anxious to restore the body of apostles to its full number, which had decreased following the defection of Judas. The disciples elected Matthias, who had known Jesus and could testify to His resurrection.

Responsorial Psalm (Ps 103): A psalm which calls on us to praise God.

Second Reading (1 Jn 4:11-16): This is one of John's most celebrated passages, full of deep theological meaning. In it he gives his simple definition of God (God is love), which has never been surpassed.

64

Third Reading (Jn 17:11-19): An important prayer of Jesus to the Father, taken from the ordination ceremony of the apostles at the Last Supper. Jesus consecrates his new priests to the Father, asking Him to protect them in the world where they must work since they are not of the world. Their task is to proclaim the truth of which the Supreme Truth is God himself.

Thought for the Day: There are two thoughts to take home with us today. First, prayer for priests that they may fulfill the vocation Christ ordained for them. The second is to make the love of God and neighbor the motivating force in our lives. In doing this we share the life of God and become most like Him.

Trinity Sunday < B

Theme: One God in three Divine Persons is a truth that requires faith. Many have tried to explain the Trinity — St. Patrick with his shamrock, the scientist with a triangle. In the end words fail and we accept the truth on the revelation of Jesus Christ.

First Reading (Dt 4:32-34, 39-40): This reading is the very heart of the Book of Deuteronomy. The experiences of the Hebrew people, Moses tells them, is unique in history, just as they are beneficiaries of a unique God and a unique revelation.

Responsorial Psalm (Ps 33): In praise of the word of the Lord.

Second Reading (Rom 8:14-17): St. Paul reminds us that we are God's own children, so much that we can speak to Him in intimacy by using the familiar *abba*. The "spirit of adoption" of which Paul speaks is the sanctifying grace the Father gives us. We are not only God's children but heirs of His kingdom.

Third Reading (Mt 28:16-20): This is the great command of Christ, the final marching orders to His Church, to which entrance is to be gained by baptism in the name of the Trinity. It is a church to which people of all nations are to be welcomed. Jesus promises that He is Emmanuel, God-with-us, an ever present power in the community of His Church.

Thought for the Day: It is Jesus Christ who makes us brothers and sisters and children of His Father. It is Jesus Christ who sends the Spirit to make us one. Although this is a feast of the unity of God, it is also a feast of our unity with the Son and Father, who are with us always.

Corpus Christi (June 13)   < B

Theme: Through the Passover seder, the Israelites recalled the mystery of the Exodus. Through the Passover meal of Christ, a new sacrament is given us that celebrates the death and resurrection of the Lord, and makes Christ truly with us.

First Reading (Ex 24:3-8): This reading gives the acceptance by the people of the covenant God offered to Israel, an acceptance sealed in blood. Moses is the mediator and confidant of God.

Responsorial Psalm (Ps 116): A hymn of thanksgiving and atonement.

Second Reading (Heb 9:11-15): Paul is contrasting the priesthood of the Old Law with that of Christ. In the Old Law the blood of goats and calves made atonement, but in the New Law it is the blood of Christ himself. In the Old Law on the Day of Atonement, the high priest would slaughter the victim outside the sanctuary and then take the blood inside to sprinkle. This was a ceremony that had to be repeated yearly. In the New Law Christ is united in the Godhead and makes one sacrifice for all eternity.

Third Reading (Mk 14:12-16, 22-26): This is Mark's account of the institution of the Eucharist during the Passover meal on Holy Thursday. This first Christian liturgy is to bring an undreamed of union with God through the body and blood of His Son.

Thought for the Day: One of the greatest benefits of liturgical reform of Vatican II is that more and more go to Holy Communion regularly. This sharing in the New Covenant is a great gift. Yet we must always be aware of our motives and not act solely from peer pressure.

Ordinary Time

Second Sunday of the Year   < B

Theme: The message of the liturgy today is one of vocation, the calling by God of each one of us to His service. For some, it is in the direct work of the Lord; for most of us, it is in serving Him with our whole hearts and minds.

First Reading (1 Sm 3:3-10, 19): The first reading relates the calling of Samuel to the vocation of prophet. It was not something he expected, but he yielded readily to God's invitation to play an important role in salvation history.

Responsorial Psalm (Ps 40): The psalmist is prepared to be open to God's voice and to do His will.

Second Reading (1 Cor 6:13-15, 17-20): The Christian vocation is not one of nature or of the flesh. Indeed, we do not even belong to ourselves as each of us was purchased by the blood of Christ. Therefore, our service is one to God.

Third Reading (Jn 1:35-42): There are echoes of both the first and second readings here. John the Baptist recognizes Jesus as the Lamb of God, someone who is to be sacrificed for others. John's own disciples are to become apostles to work in the direct ministry of Jesus. After this contact Jesus begins to form His religious community.

Thought for the Day: The Christian vocation is given to us in baptism. It is one that we can reject but never totally escape. God's will exists for each of us. We must determine what that will is for us. Once we recognize the will, we cannot turn back because our ultimate judgment depends upon how we respond.

Third Sunday of the Year   < B

Theme: The basic note of the readings today is one of conversion. Paul reminds us to order our values properly, for those of the world are but temporal and fleeting.

First Reading (Jon 3:1-5, 10): The book of Jonah is full of unlikely surprises. God sends Jonah to preach repentance to a pagan people. With the bad example of the Jews in mind, Jonah considers his mission hopeless. He does God's will anyway and the unexpected happens — the Ninevites repent and do God's will. Jonah is upset by his success.

Responsorial Psalm (Ps 25): God does not abandon sinners but seeks always to persuade them to His law.

Second Reading (1 Cor 7:29-31): Everything in this world is passing. If we realize this, we will put our values where they belong. Paul seems to be echoing Christ's own challenge: "What does it profit a man if he gains the whole world and suffers the loss of his soul?"

Third Reading (Mk 1:14-20): In this reading from Mark one gets some idea of the personal majesty and magnetism Jesus possessed. Jesus comes demanding reformation of lives and full adherence to the Good News He preaches. His simple invitation is commanding enough for Peter, James, John and Andrew to leave settled careers and follow Him into the unknown. These conversions are all the more overwhelming for lack of dramatics.

Thought for the Day: Christ is challenging each of us to give up our present way, repent and change. For too many, though, the cares and diversions of the world drown out His invitation. We accept the fact of our baptism and fail to reflect on its implications. All of us are given the opportunity to make an informed commitment to Christ, but few respond.

Fourth Sunday of the Year   < B

Theme: God promised His people that he would not leave them without leadership. He would send them prophets to guide them. The greatest of the prophets was to be Jesus Christ, His own Son.

First Reading (Dt 18:15-20): Up until the time of Moses, God intervened directly in salvation history. Although God appeared in different forms to Moses, the Jews were terrified by these apparitions, believing that no one should approach the great sanctity of the Lord. God promised that in the future He would communicate with them and direct them through prophets.

Responsorial Psalm (Ps 95): The Lord is near to all who call on Him. We must accept His word and harden not our hearts as the Israelites did to the revelations of their leader Moses.

Second Reading (1 Cor 7:32-35): Paul continues his letter to the Corinthians by taking up the subject of marriage and virginity. Paul recognizes that a celibate and virgin life is not for all, but he gives some reasons why he considers it a higher state of life.

Third Reading (Mk 1:21-28): Christ was the great prophet, the absolute bringer of salvation, who taught with a recognizable authority. A prophet is an envoy from God, mandated in his vocation by God, a bearer of revelation, one who lives in obedience to God's laws. Christ filled these qualifications in a supreme manner. His unique character was recognized by the people and was testified to even by unclean spirits over whom He had authority.

Thought for the Day: Some today try to bring God down to their level, to make religion a sort of buddy affair. But God has supreme majesty and dignity; before Him we must always bend our knee. It is only through Christ that He becomes understandable in human terms.

Fifth Sunday of the Year   < B

Theme: Although the liturgists have tried to give the readings of each week a common theme, sometimes it is not easy to find. At first glance, the readings today may seem disjointed. There is however a theme: One must make efforts in the daily tasks of life.

First Reading (Job 7:1-4, 6-7): This is a rather gloomy reading by a man whose encounter with God was very personal and emotional. Job never loses confidence in God despite all his troubles, but he does not anticipate an afterlife and sometimes wonders whether his suffering is worth all his pain and agony.

Responsorial Psalm (Ps 147): An answer to Job's doubts. God does heal the brokenhearted and He does care.

Second Reading (1 Cor 9:16-19, 22-23): Paul cannot and does not want to escape his vocation to preach the Gospel. He becomes all things to all men so that his work might be effective.

Third Reading (Mk 1:29-39): Mark gives us in capsule form a twenty-four-hour period in the life of Jesus, during which we see Him preaching, teaching, praying and curing. He is a man who likes solitude, yet this will be something that will increasingly be denied Him.

Thought for the Day: Jesus went off to a lonely place to pray. The fact that encounters with God in the Bible are in lonely places — the desert or a mountaintop — should tell us something. It is very difficult to hear God in the crowded tumults of life. Each one of us must withdraw into the lonely places within us and there speak to God, and, more important, listen.

Sixth Sunday of the Year   < B

Theme: While the main consideration of today's readings would seem to be leprosy, it is in reality sin and Christ's power to forgive sin.

First Reading (Lv 13:1-2, 44-46). The Mosaic law regarding lepers was a harsh one: complete separation from the community. This was probably done for fear of contagion, but the Jews also looked upon leprosy as a punishment for sin. Just as there was an uncleanness in death, so this living death made a person unclean.

Responsorial Psalm (Ps 32): The psalmist expresses the real meaning of this liturgy: "Happy is he whose fault is taken away."

Second Reading (1 Cor 10:31 — 11:1): Everything we do in life should be done for God's glory. A simple intention when we arise can make every act of our day a prayer.

Third Reading (Mk 1:40-45): A leper approaches Jesus in great faith, telling Him that Jesus can cure him if He wishes. Jesus cures the man of his leprosy. Through this miracle, Jesus was demonstrating His power not only over bodily ills but also over sin. Jesus meets evil head on and is victorious.

Thought for the Day: Sin is a spiritual leprosy. What sin does to the soul is far worse than what the untreated ravages of leprosy can do to the body. Yet if we should ever fall into sin, we know that Christ is ready to cure us through the Sacrament of Penance. His mercy reaches out for us if we will but meet Him.

Seventh Sunday of the Year   < B

Theme: Because we do not see the crippling effects of sin, we do not realize what a moral disorder it is. Yet God's love will save us from the crippling effects of sin if we will accept it.

First Reading (Is 43:18-19, 21-22, 24-25): Although God's love worked many wonders for the people of Israel in their great Exodus from Egypt, they nevertheless doubted God and sinned against Him. Isaiah reminds us that God was ready with His forgiveness and willing to forget their offenses.

Responsorial Psalm (Ps 41): The Lord God is ready to make us whole both physically and spiritually.

Second Reading (2 Cor 1:18-22): Paul has been accused of duplicity in changing his plans about visiting Corinth. He refutes the charge, saying that God's faithfulness is the source of his own constancy.

Third Reading (Mk 2:1-12): There is a sub-theme that runs through Mark which says that conflict between Jesus and the Jewish authorities will result in His death. This Gospel is the first example given by Mark. However, the liturgy uses this passage for its second part which shows the power of Jesus over sin and sickness. Once the power of Satan is removed, the paralytic is cured.

Thought for the Day: While Jesus can cure the ills of the body, His greatest gift to us is healing from sin. Jesus clearly gives a demonstration of this power in healing the paralytic. It is a promise to us that we can be saved from eternal death if we will but repent and seek the salvation of the Lord.

Eighth Sunday of the Year   < B

Theme: God wishes to save that which is lost. His tender concern for the people of Israel culminates in the mission of His Son through which God will make His new and lasting covenant.

First Reading (Hos 2:16-17, 21-22): God's pursuit of the people of Israel is symbolized in Hosea's portrait of Israel as an unfaithful wife. This passage compares the honeymoon of the first days of Israel in the desert during Exodus and its later unfaithfulness of seeking false gods. Yet God will espouse Israel in a new covenant.

Responsorial Psalm (Ps 103): Mercy is another name for God.

Second Reading (2 Cor 3:1-6): The Spirit is the life-giving force of the New Covenant. The rigorism of the Old Law has been replaced, and the New Law lives in the hearts of those who are open to the life of the Spirit.

Third Reading (Mk 2:18-22): Mark stresses the fact that the messianic age has arrived. John the Baptist was a link between the old and the new; therefore, he preached a baptism of penance, suitable to a waiting or a preparation. Now that Christ has arrived the old is ended, as is the usefulness of old wineskins. The time of preparation is over, the marriage feast has begun.

Thought for the Day: The Old Testament was a time of betrothal, but in the New we respond to the presence of the bridegroom. We have been freed and transformed in Christ. We put aside the old things that hinder us from following Christ and live the new life which He has brought to us.

Ninth Sunday of the Year   < B

Theme: Keep holy the Sabbath day.

First Reading (Dt 5:12-15): The Book of Deuteronomy contains the laws by which the tribes of Israel were to live. At the top of these laws were the commandments given to Moses during the Exodus, the chief of which was honor due God. This honor was shown by setting one day aside for Him.

Responsorial Psalm (Ps 81): There is only one true God, He who brought Israel out of Egypt.

Second Reading (2 Cor 4:6-11): The light of Christ shines through Paul's acts so that others may be led to Jesus. This has led to persecution and even threats of death, but this does not unduly concern him because we are supposed to die to self anyway.

Third Reading (Mk 2:23-3:6): By the time of Jesus the Sabbath laws had become very legalistic and confining, so much so that their purpose was lost. Jesus shows that He has authority to change these laws when common sense demands. It was this attitude that the Apostles remembered when they changed the Christian Sabbath to Sunday.

Thought for the Day: From earliest Christian times, Sunday has been set aside as a day of rest consecrated to the worship of God. The Church legislates that all Catholics must participate in the Eucharistic Celebration on Sundays and Holy Days unless they are legitimately excused.

Tenth Sunday of the Year   < B

Theme: Obedience to God's law is in the last analysis the only way we prove our love for Him.

First Reading (Gn 3:9-15): The Genesis story of the fall of Adam and Eve is a failure in obedience to God. It also shows how we try to escape the consequences of our acts. Adam blames Eve for his sin, and Eve blames the serpent. Nevertheless, through free will we are responsible for our own sins.

Responsorial Psalm (Ps 130): The *De Profundis* is one of the great penitential psalms of the Church. It is a cry for mercy with confidence in forgiveness.

Second Reading (2 Cor 4:13 — 5:1): Life is transitory, but there is that within each one of us that is eternal. We look not, therefore, to the passing things of the world but to the everlasting home which is to come.

Third Reading (Mk 3:20-35): The mother of Jesus and some relatives come to see Jesus. He replies that those who are close to Him are those who do God's will. The inference is that the scribes who are criticizing Him are opposing the will of God. It may also be an oblique rebuke to some of His relatives who did not understand His mission.

Thought for the Day: So many Christians give lip service to God. They may faithfully attend Mass, recite the prayers and sing the hymns, but their lives are self-centered. "None of those who cry out, 'Lord, Lord,' will enter the kingdom of God, but only the one who does the will of my Father in heaven."

Eleventh Sunday of the Year   < B

Theme: The Church of Christ is like a great tree. It begins as a small seed but grows mighty, sheltering all the people of the world.

First Reading (Ez 17:22-24): The cedar trees of Lebanon were greatly prized for their fragrant wood. Ezekiel makes an allegory of the cedar for the messianic restoration.

Responsorial Psalm (Ps 92): The just will grow strong like a cedar of Lebanon.

Second Reading (2 Cor 5:6-10): There is a reference here to the particular judgment when each of us will get what we deserve, based on the merits gained in life.

Third Reading (Mk 4:26-34): The two parables here stress growth from small beginnings. God's kingdom grows the same way — from humble beginnings to greatness. There is also a universality in the parable of the mustard seed with the birds representing all the peoples of the world.

Thought for the Day: The powers of the world of Jesus paid little respect to Him, never imagining the great movement that would grow from His death. The cedar of Lebanon is an image of the Church, great and strong, sheltering all nations in one worship of God.

Twelfth Sunday of the Year   < B

Theme: Anyone who watches the raw power of the sea in a storm realizes that it is beyond human control. Only God, the creator of the universe, has greater power.

First Reading (Job 38:1, 8-11): In the ancient mind, the sea was a malevolent and uncontrollable force. Out of a storm, God speaks to Job, justifying His actions and explaining His nature. Who but God could put boundaries to the sea and hold its might in sway?

Responsorial Psalm (Ps 106): God protects from the menace of the deep, saving sailors by stilling the raging storm.

Second Reading (2 Cor 5:14-17): Christ has brought about through His death a new creation. The Christian lives no longer for him or her self but for Christ and His brothers and sisters.

Third Reading (Mk 4:35-41): Today's first reading and psalm prepare us for the Gospel. "Who can this be," the Gospel asks, "that the wind and the sea obey Him?" There can only be one answer. It is God.

Thought for the Day: It is easier for us to control the power of the sea than plumb the unfathomable depths of God. The boy whom St. Augustine found trying to empty the Mediterranean Sea with his pail would have had an easier time than we would trying to comprehend the infinite with finite minds. Is it completely hopeless? No. As Jesus told Philip: "Whoever has seen me has seen the Father." Jesus Christ we can understand because He shares our nature and through Him we know God.

Thirteenth Sunday of the Year   < B

Theme: Death is the major theme of the liturgy today. The Old Testament reminds us that God does not will death but it has come as a result of man's sin. Jesus is the conqueror of death and will raise all men to everlasting life.

First Reading (Wis 1:13-15; 2:23-24): This reading from the Book of Wisdom sounds almost as if it came from St. Paul and shows its influence on Pauline thinking. It tells of the tragedy caused by original sin, and the writer suggests that even more terrible than physical death is spiritual death. God's justice is undying.

Responsorial Psalm (Ps 30): A hymn of thanksgiving for rescue from great peril.

Second Reading (2 Cor 8:7, 9, 13-15): Paul is calling on the relatively affluent Church in Corinth to assist the needy brethren in Jerusalem. The thought behind this reading has application today when Christians of the industrialized nations are called to assist those in developing countries.

Third Reading (Mk 5:21-43): Jesus raises a dead girl to life. While Mark interprets this miracle as an act to convince His apostles as to who He really is, it does show His power over death, which He will dramatically demonstrate again in His own resurrection.

Thought for the Day: There is much talk today about death and dying because it is one of the deepest problems of life. Some believers blame God, but as Wisdom reminds us, God did not make death. For most in the world, death is a tragic conclusion — a finality which man dumbly must accept. For the Christian, however, death speaks of the significance of life where only sin can cause real death and where earthly passing is but a prelude to eternal life.

Fourteenth Sunday of the Year   < B

Theme: "A prophet has no honor in his own country." This observation of Christ has echo in all three readings today. Israel rejected the prophets. The Jewish establishment rejected Jesus. How do we regard those who serve a prophetic function among us today?

First Reading (Ex 2:2-5): As do all of the prophets of the Old Testament, Ezekiel recounts his call by God, how he was called to be God's interpreter and sent to preach to his fellow captives in Babylonia. All the prophets establish their credentials.

Responsorial Psalm (Ps 123): A song begging God's mercy on his oppressed servants. It is an echo of exiles.

Second Reading (2 Cor 12:7-10): Paul speaks of a chronic affliction he has. Like Jesus in Gethsemane, he has begged God three times to remove it. God's reply was that His grace was sufficient to guarantee Paul's success as an apostle. This weakness, along with the persecutions he suffers, makes him strong.

Third Reading (Mk 6:1-6): Jesus returns home to Nazareth. His reputation and the fame of His miracles preceded Him. The townsfolk expect more miracles, not understanding that Jesus only worked miracles in response to faith in himself, which is lacking in the people of Nazareth, who perhaps from envy look upon Him as ordinary.

Thought for the Day: The question posed by the people of Nazareth: "Where did this man get all this?" might be our own. If the power of Jesus comes from God, then God sanctions all that He says, including His Sonship.

Fifteenth Sunday of the Year   < B

Theme: The liturgy today shows people responding to God's call — Amos to prophesy, the apostles to carry God's message of repentance. All of us have a calling (vocation) to some state in life, and some God calls directly into His service.

First Reading (Am 7:12-15): Amos was a shepherd and dresser of trees when God called him and sent him to the royal sanctuary at Bethel, where the envy of the priest Amaziah brought opposition. This did not bother Amos, who seemed to have independent means. He prophesied an invasion of the northern kingdom, during which Amaziah's wife would be barbarously treated, his children killed and his lands confiscated.

Responsorial Psalm (Ps 85): The Lord proclaims peace and justice.

Second Reading (Eph 1:3-14): God chose us before the world began and He predestined us through Jesus Christ to be His adopted sons. God bestows on us all riches of graces.

Third Reading (Mk 6:7-13): Christ sends His apostles out on their first mission. They are not yet to preach the fullness of His teaching — that will come after the Resurrection. Now they are to proclaim a Gospel of repentance. An interesting sidelight here is the note that the Sacrament of Anointing of the Sick was already in use.

Thought for the Day: God knows the needs of His Church and is certainly calling those needed to serve Him as priests, brothers and sisters. Unfortunately, there is much din that crowds out His voice. The world besieges us on every side and even inside the Church there are those who spread doubt and confusion. We need to withdraw to a lonely place to hear the call of God.

Sixteenth Sunday of the Year   < B

Theme: Jesus is the promise of the ages, the true shepherd sent by God to teach His people the way to peace.

First Reading (Jer 23:1-6): Jeremiah accuses the kings of Israel for being false shepherds who have allowed God's people to be scattered. He predicts that the people will be brought back from exile and a new and true shepherd will arise from the line of David.

Responsorial Psalm (Ps 23): A popular psalm which proclaims the Lord as shepherd who will provide all that is needed.

Second Reading (Eph 2:13-18): Paul states his doctrine of Christ as peacemaker. Through His sacrifice Jesus the Messiah enables the people to make peace with themselves and, at the same time, He draws the Jews and the Gentiles together so that everyone everywhere can reach God through the Holy Spirit.

Third Reading (Mk 6:30-34): The theme of Jeremiah is applied directly to Christ. Seeking solitude, Jesus finds that the crowds have followed Him. He sees a people hungry for instruction "like sheep without a shepherd." So He begins to teach them and prepare them for the doctrine of the Eucharist.

Thought for the Day: Jesus Christ was the Good Shepherd who had come to lead His people. His work did not end with His crucifixion but continues to this day. The hunger for peace and justice which drove the people to follow Christ is still present in our world. People today are like sheep without a shepherd. The teaching of Christ is the bread for the world's hunger, and it must be brought to the waiting millions.

Seventeenth Sunday of the Year   < B

Theme: While the obvious theme is the feeding of the hungry, an obligation on all Christians, humanity hungers not only for bread but also for the Word of God. The Body of Christ is the true bread we must offer to our brothers and sisters. This is also the theme for the next two Sundays.

First Reading (2 Kgs 4:42-44): The student of the Bible cannot help but notice the parallels that exist between the Old and New Testaments. God foreshadowed so many things which were to come. Elisha's multiplication of the barley loaves anticipated a similar miracle of Christ.

Responsorial Psalm (Ps 145): The hand of the Lord feeds us because He is near to all who call upon Him.

Second Reading (Eph 4:1-6): This great Pauline passage emphasizes the unity of God with His creation. Paul tells us that there is but one body, one Lord, one faith, one baptism.

Third Reading (Jn 6:1-15): Jesus parallels Elisha's miracle in a far greater degree. He feeds a crowd of five thousand with a few barley loaves and a couple of fish. Impressed, the crowd proclaims Jesus the promised prophet and would make Him king.

Thought for the Day: Christ's miracles were worked for the furtherance of His mission. While ostensibly today's miracle was to satisfy the hunger of the crowd, it was in the divine plan a

78

direct preparation for the announcement of the doctrine of the Eucharist. It was as if Jesus was saying, "See, if I can multiply these loaves and fish, do not be surprised when I say I can multiply myself."

Eighteenth Sunday of the Year   <   B

Theme: The Eucharist is of central importance in Christian life. Foreshadowed in the Old Testament, it came to fruition in the sacrifice of Christ.

First Reading (Ex 16:2-4, 12-15): Although the Jews should have been elated and trustful in God, particularly after their miraculous passage through the Red Sea, they soon began to complain about the lack of food in the Sinai desert. They even wished that they were back in Egyptian slavery. God told Moses that He would care for His people by sending them food from heaven called manna.

Responsorial Psalm (Ps 78): In this song of praise the psalmist reminds the people that God gave them bread from heaven to sustain them in the Exodus.

Second Reading (Eph 4:17, 20-24): Paul again reminds his readers that a total conversion to Christianity is needed. "Put on the new man," he tells us. Most of us have grown up in a cultural Christianity and therefore each of us should have a perfect conversion.

Third Reading (Jn 6:24-35): Jesus, through His miracle of the multiplication of the loaves and fishes, is preparing the minds of His followers for the doctrine of the Eucharist. Following the miracle, Jesus tells His disciples that He is the bread from heaven sent down from the Father. The disciples take this symbolically, but shortly Jesus shall tell them the Eucharist will be no symbol but actuality.

Thought for the Day: St. Paul calls on us to assess ourselves. Providing daily bread for our families is an important and necessary goal. Yet even those with all the material comforts yearn for something more. This desire is for the Bread of Life, which can cure all of our spiritual hunger. Let us resolve then to receive the Eucharist whenever possible.

Nineteenth Sunday of the Year   < B

Theme: The Eucharist is necessary for spiritual life. The body and blood of Jesus are the food all must partake to maintain this spiritual life.

First Reading (1 Kgs 19:4-8): The great major prophet Elijah fought against idolatry, seemingly in vain. Unchecked by the people and persecuted by the wicked Queen Jezebel, Elijah flees into the wilderness in despondency. God miraculously provides him with food before sending him on to Mt. Sinai.

Responsorial Psalm (Ps 34): God protects those who call on Him, and His goodness is ours for the asking.

Second Reading (Eph 4:30 — 5:2): Paul continues his teaching on the necessity of conversion to Christ. We should imitate God in every way we can but primarily by living a life of love for God and neighbor. It does no good belonging to Christ's Church unless we live up to its teachings.

Third Reading (Jn 6:41-51): All of the preparation is now finished. The preaching and miracles prepared His followers for the stupendous announcement that if one is to have life, he or she must eat the flesh of Christ and drink His blood. The Jews knew Christ was not talking in symbols, yet despite their long preparation they turned away and could follow Him no longer. They could not accept the Eucharist.

Thought for the Day: All of us at one time have experienced the dejection of Elijah and feared we did not have strength to finish our journey through life. Just as God strengthened Elijah by heavenly food to continue his journey to Sinai, we too have such a food and help in the Eucharist.

Twentieth Sunday of the Year   < B

Theme: The Eucharist is the very core of Christian life. In the Eucharist, Christ is made physically present to us. This knowledge about Christ is the greatest wisdom we can have.

First Reading (Prv 9:1-6): While this reading has been chosen for its eucharistic reference to the banquet of wisdom, its application is broader. It is wisdom that leads us to God's banquet and enables us to see what is truly valuable and what is dross.

Responsorial Psalm (Ps 34): This is a psalm with eucharistic application, inviting us to taste and see the goodness of the Lord.

Second Reading (Eph 5:15-20): Paul is making a plea for Christian behavior. Wise behavior consists in knowing God's will and doing it.

Third Reading (Jn 6:51-58): Jesus' great eucharistic discourse follows the miracle of the multiplication of the loaves and the fishes, which was a preparatory act for the doctrine He now teaches. In this section of the discourse Jesus speaks of the necessity of the Eucharist and the fact that the eucharistic miracle is really His flesh and blood, the partaking of which gives eternal life.

Thought for the Day: The Mass is the core of Christian life. In the Eucharist it is Christ himself giving worship to the Father for us. In the Mass we join with Christ in offering himself to the Father once again for mankind. We must guard that our Communions do not become routine, remembering always the Divine Person we offer and receive.

Twenty-first Sunday of the Year   < B

Theme: Faith is not static and must be continually renewed. We stand in need of constant conversion, of giving ourselves to Christ.

First Reading (Jos 24:1-2, 15-18): Joshua was the successor of Moses. He was to lead the people into the promised land. At Shechem he gathered all the people of Israel before him and asked them if they were prepared to serve only Yahweh. The people reaffirmed their covenant with God. With the covenant renewed, the people entered the Promised Land.

Responsorial Psalm (Ps 34): A hymn of praise to God's goodness.

Second Reading (Eph 5:21-32): This reading from St. Paul is not popular with many women, yet we must remember it was the Holy Spirit directing through Paul the different duties of husband and wife. St. Paul is saying that a family can have only one head, the husband, to whom the wife owes certain duties. The husband, in turn, has the obligation of loving his wife. Paul likens marriage to the Church, of which Jesus Christ is the head.

Third Reading (Jn 6:60-69): This reading tells of the effects of Christ's sermon on the Eucharist. Many of His followers turned away and left Him. His apostles remained because their faith in Jesus was complete. Peter's response indicates this. He and the other apostles have come to believe that Jesus is the Son of God.

Thought for the Day: We are all challenged from time to time to make a choice between the values of the world and the values of Christ. Each time we choose those of Jesus we strengthen our Christian conversion, realizing that there is nothing worthwhile in the values of the world. Christ often asks us, "Will you also leave me?" What answer do we make?

Twenty-second Sunday of the Year   <   B

Theme: Our commitment to Jesus must take first place in our lives. It is a commitment that lasts forever. It is not a legalistic commitment but one that comes from the heart.

First Reading (Dt 4:1-2, 6, 8): Moses is the mediator between God and the people of Israel. It is his task to instruct them in the commandments of God. As long as Israel obeys God, it will prosper. The law given by Moses is different from all other laws since it has come from God himself. Therefore, it must be obeyed freely.

Responsorial Psalm (Ps 15): Our obedience to the law should be in full compliance.

Second Reading (Jas 1:17-18, 21-22, 27): Everything worthwhile comes to us from God. His work is our life. The word is not one merely to be said, but it must be lived. As St. James tells us, "Act on this word. If all you do is listen to it, you are deceiving yourselves." How often do we hear the word preached and do nothing more?

Third Reading (Mk 7:1-8, 14-15, 21-23): Christ tells the crowd that they must give more than lip service. Then he turns to a subject that is often forgotten. Internal sins are more terrible than external acts. Every sin comes from within, and one must guard against evil inclinations.

Thought for the Day: Too many people believe that sin is committed only when it is done in act. Christ tells us that our interior dispositions will be judged. All sin is first presented by the intellect and then given consent by the will. We must keep control of our internal senses to be truly united to Christ.

Twenty-third Sunday of the Year   < B

Theme: Jesus makes the deaf to hear and the dumb to speak, thus fulfilling the prophets. There are various types of dumbness and deafness which we can develop and which Jesus can cure for us.

First Reading (Is 35:4-7): Isaiah promises the Israelites that they will not be neglected by God. In this beautiful prophecy we can find a spiritual meaning referring to Christ.

Responsorial Psalm (Ps 146): The psalm repeats the message of Isaiah in almost the same words. God does not forget the oppressed.

Second Reading (Jas 2:1-5): St. James recognizes the fact that there will always be rich and poor, but he emphasizes that before God all are equal. There should be no discrimination in the Church. James tells us that the poor are God's special elect and in the eternal view they are really the rich.

Third Reading (Mk 7:31-37): Mark tells us of two miracles by Christ. He views them as means of opening the minds and hearts of His apostles. Jesus is building up to the confirmation of Peter as head of His Church, and these miracles are to strengthen the belief of His followers in Him.

Thought for the Day: How often do we bow down to those with riches or power and cultivate those of social stature! Yet James warns us we must treat everyone equally. Those whom the world honors already have their reward. The used and abused people of the world are the ones Christ will first befriend. We must actively support the dignity and rights of the poor and weak. God will reward us for this.

Twenty-fourth Sunday of the Year   < B

Theme: Jesus had been gradually preparing the minds of His apostles through His teaching and miracles. Now He begins to reveal the secrets that will scandalize some. Ahead lies suffering and a kingdom not of this world.

First Reading (Is 50:5-9): Isaiah paints a portrait of the suffering servant. The servant is not received by the people who torment and persecute him, but he remains firm in his confidence in God.

Responsorial Psalm (Ps 116): The psalmist gives praise to God, who rescues him.

Second Reading (Jas 2:14-18): Faith without good works means nothing more than a personal sterility. If we believe, we must act. One who proclaims belief in Jesus Christ and does nothing to help his poorer brothers in need is following himself. Fraternal charity is the true test of Christianity.

Third Reading (Mk 8:27-35): Christ's efforts have been leading up to this climactic moment. He now directly asks His closest followers who He is. Peter gives the immediate reply, "You are the Messiah." Jesus then reveals that His kingdom is not of this world and that there is much He will have to suffer. Some of His followers protest, thinking He is to be a worldly king. Even Peter is rebuked for his misunderstanding.

Thought for the Day: This challenging section of Mark's Gospel should be meditated on frequently. It is an assessment of our human values. We can react with the doubts of the apostles, seek a worldly kingdom, or go beyond and discover that God's values are entirely different.

Twenty-fifth Sunday of the Year   < B

Theme: Jesus continues to prepare His apostles for His coming passion. Thinking in terms of an earthly kingdom, they do not understand Him. There is still a lack of faith here.

First Reading (Wis 2:12, 17-20): This is a strong reading. The author gives voice to the wicked who plot against the good man. These words are almost the same as those who plotted the death of Jesus. They are the words of the unbeliever, the atheist.

Responsorial Psalm (Ps 54): A plea for God for protection against one's foes.

Second Reading (Jas 3:16-4:3): James makes a number of points in this reading, but the important one is that peace is the fruit of justice. Conflicts, quarrels, disputes, envy, all these come from injustice.

Third Reading (Mk 9:30-37): There is a twofold lesson in today's reading. Again Jesus foretells His passion and death in an effort to prepare His followers, who do not comprehend His words and who not only think of an earthly kingdom but what roles they will play in it. Jesus tells them His kingdom is not of this world and that the highest places in it will go to those who serve others, not themselves.

Thought for the Day: It is not easy for us to understand the Cross. To the world it is a foolish, stupid gesture. Yet it was a triumph of love and the conquest over evil. Suffering, to be understood, must be viewed through Christian eyes. Then for us, as for so many saints, will it take on true meaning.

Twenty-sixth Sunday of the Year < B

Theme: Following Christ means sacrifice, often sacrificing something we esteem highly. Jesus tells us that nothing is worth the loss of heaven.

First Reading (Nm 11:25-29): Moses feels the burden of his office, and God gives him seventy elders to help him. These men have extraordinary gifts. Far from being envious, Moses wishes that all Israelites had these gifts.

Responsorial Psalm (Ps 19): The law of the Lord is perfect.

Second Reading (Jas 5:1-6): This is undoubtedly the most direct and strongest passage on social justice to be found in the New Testament. James attacks the rich in strong terms because they put worldly values before those of God. The day of retribution will come.

Third Reading (Mk 9:38-43, 47, 48): Christ expects His followers to go the whole way for Him even if it means doing away with something we highly value. Our worldly loves can give scandal, and if this is the case it would have been better if we had never been born.

Thought for the Day: Pride and self-gratification are our chief barriers to complete service to God. They show a sense of disordered values. No sacrifice is too great to rid ourselves of those things that lead us from God. Jesus uses strong examples to emphasize the requirement of total devotion to His Father.

Twenty-seventh Sunday of the Year   < B

Theme: The sacredness and unity of Christian marriage is the subject of today's liturgy. Christ minces no words in forbidding divorce.

First Reading (Gn 2:18-24): The Genesis story of the creation of man and woman is simply told. The writer expresses the deep unity of marriage where husband and wife are no longer two but one body.

Responsorial Psalm (Ps 128): This beautiful psalm, often used in the marriage ceremony, expresses the deeply held marriage philosophy of the Jews.

Second Reading (Heb 2:9-11): There is a deep theology hidden in today's reading. In assuming human flesh to become our Brother, Jesus made himself a little lower than the angels. By His death He identified completely with us. For all of this He is exalted most highly by the Father.

Third Reading (Mk 10:2-16): In this teaching on divorce, Jesus deliberately departs from the Mosaic tradition. He minces no words but speaks clearly and forcibly. Because of these words of Christ, the Church cannot admit divorce or admit divorced and remarried Catholics to the sacraments. This is one of the hard sayings of Christianity, which makes no pretense of being an easy religion.

Thought for the Day: Marriage is under siege today, and many live openly in concubinage. Divorce is rampant in our society. Marriage laws are not a matter of Church discipline but come from Christ himself. The Church can do nothing but obey the words of Christ.

Twenty-eighth Sunday of the Year   < B

Theme: The theme of today's Mass might well be a contrast between wisdom and riches. In the ultimate reality, riches really count for nothing.

First Reading (Wis 7:7-11): To Solomon, nothing in the world was the equal of wisdom. In today's reading he tells how he prefers wisdom over his kingship, and deems riches as nothing in comparison to wisdom. Wisdom is really a gift of the Holy Spirit, which enables us to judge rightly in all that pertains to life and conduct, particularly our relationship to God.

Responsorial Psalm (Ps 90): A song to wisdom.

Second Reading (Heb 4:12-13): The Word of God sees into our innermost intentions and nothing can be hidden from Him.

Third Reading: (Mk 10:17-30): This is a Gospel concerned with perfection. Jesus tells the young man that it is not enough to keep the commandments, that to follow Him means to go the whole way, even giving up his riches. Jesus uses the young man's refusal as the occasion to explain to His apostles how difficult it is for people attached to worldly goods to enter heaven. "Then who can be saved?" ask the apostles. Jesus indicates that God looks into the heart and then makes His judgment.

Thought for the Day: The Gospel today presents a problem for every Christian. How do we apply it to our situation in life when we are surrounded by so many material comforts which we now consider necessities, although a few years ago they were thought of as luxuries? The answer lies in our mental attitude toward them. Are we attached to them more than we are attached to Christ and His Church?

Twenty-ninth Sunday of the Year   < B

Theme: Suffering is the dominant note of today's liturgy.

First Reading (Is 53:10-11): Isaiah speaks of the suffering servant. The key part of the reading is: "Through his suffering, my servant shall justify many, and their guilt he shall bear." These words apply directly to Christ.

Responsorial Psalm (Ps 33): We can put our confidence in the word of the Lord.

Second Reading (Heb 4:14-16): Here is Paul's great hymn of praise to Jesus Christ, our High Priest, one who thoroughly knows the heart of man.

Third Reading (Mk 10:35-45): This Gospel has a short and long form. In the first part, James and John ask for the major share in Christ's kingdom. They are still thinking in earthly terms of worldly power. Jesus' reply is surprising. He promises them that they will suffer with Him. In the second part of the Gospel, Jesus calls all His apostles together, probably as the result of the request of Zebedee's sons, and tells them that theirs is to be a life of service. He tells them that He himself has come on earth not to be served but to serve.

Thought for the Day: Christianity is not a personal, Jesus-and-I religion, but a religion of service, particularly to those in need. The greatest needs are those of the spirit. The main part of our judgment will come, not on personal sins, but on how well we have served those children of God who are in need.

Thirtieth Sunday of the Year   < B

Theme: Jesus came to restore God's people to the Father. The blind man exhibits the attitude each of us should have of opening ourselves to God's grace.

First Reading (Jer 31:7-9): In 721 B.C., the northern kingdom of Israel was destroyed and its people sent into exile. A century later Jeremiah tells the exiles they are as dear to God as a first-born son and that they will be restored in joy to their homeland.

Responsorial Psalm (Ps 126): A prayer to God to end Israel's exile.

Second Reading (Heb 5:1-6): St. Paul tells us what a true priest is. God alone chooses him from among men, just as He picked Aaron and his descendants to be priests of the Old Law. The priest offers sacrifice for the forgiveness of sin, his own as well as those of the people. Christ is our high priest. It is God's own Son who identifies himself with our human condition and raises it to new life.

Third Reading (Mk 10:46-50): As Christ is preparing His triumphal entry into Jerusalem, the blind Bartimaeus begs for sight and is cured. Jesus uses the incident to show what should be happening in the faith of His followers. It will take faith to remain firm in the face of the sufferings and tragedies that lie at the end of the week.

Thought for the Day: Because of the moral confusion today, Christians are in great need of faith. Yet faith is not an end, only the point of departure. We must continually ask the Master,

"Lord, that I may see!" We are called upon to renew our minds and hearts, always acting out of our love for Christ.

Thirty-first Sunday of the Year   < B

Theme: We must make complete commitment to God. This is the source of every commandment, whether of the Old or New Law. Because Christ is our high priest, the New Law has come into being. We must accept God's Word, which is Jesus Christ.

First Reading (Dt 6:2-6): Moses summarizes all the commandments into one Great Law: Love the Lord, your God, with all your heart, soul and strength; in other words, make a total commitment to Him.

Responsorial Psalm (Ps 18): A hymn of the king in thanksgiving to God.

Second Reading (Heb 7:23-28): We are at the heart of Paul's doctrinal letter to the Hebrews. He contrasts the old priesthood with that of Christ. Jesus was perfect, the savior of all, chosen by God because of His sacrifice as our eternal high priest. Whereas the priests of old were weak men, our new high priest is the Son of God himself.

Third Reading (Mk 12:28-34): Like Moses, Jesus summarizes the law. He tells the scribe who is concerned about the relative importance of the 600 precepts of Jewish law that all of these regulations can be reduced to one word: love — love of God and love of neighbor. In instructing the scribe, He instructs His own disciples and each one of us.

Thought for the Day: Jesus did not end the Ten Commandments, but He summarized them in a positive word: love. If we love God we will serve and honor Him. If we love God, we will love His creation, particularly all people, whom He created in His own likeness. Jesus invites us to change our thinking and to accept His teachings.

Thirty-second Sunday of the Year   < B

Theme: There is a social caste to today's liturgy. Widows are a scriptural type for the defenseless poor who remain loyal to God despite their condition. God rewards their love.

First Reading (1 Kgs 17:10-16): Elijah, God's prophet, asks a widow woman for food. Despite the fact that it is a time of famine and she has only a handful of food, she shares it. Thereafter, she has abundant food. God's blessing on her charity is obvious.

Responsorial Psalm (Ps 146): A hymn of praise to God, who nourishes the oppressed and poor.

Second Reading (Heb 9:24-28): The sacrifice of Christ is eternal and lasting. The sacrifice of the Old Law had to be repeated again and again. Because Jesus is the Son of God, His sacrifice is infinite and He needed to die only once.

Third Reading (Mk 12:38-44): Jesus praises the widow's mite as being greater than the contributions of the wealthy. Jesus could not stand hypocrisy. He uses this occasion to rebuke the scribes, who are concerned with appearances but do not hesitate to "devour the savings of widows."

Thought for the Day: Jesus clearly indicates that His values differ greatly from the world's. It is not wealth and prestige that impress Him but poverty and charity. We do not judge a gift by its size and value but by the spirit in which it is offered.

Thirty-third Sunday of the Year   < **B**

Theme: As we reach the end of the Church year, our attention is focused on the end of the world and the promise of everlasting life for God's elect.

First Reading (Dn 12:1-3): This passage is unusual because it is one of the very few Old Testament readings that give evidence of the resurrection of the dead. Written among the Jews in exile, Daniel looks ahead to the end of the world, when the Archangel Michael will protect God's people.

Responsorial Psalm (Ps 16): A prayer of trust that God will enable His followers to conquer death.

Second Reading (Heb 10:11-14): By the single offering of His life, Christ has achieved the eternal perfection of all those whom He is sanctifying. His sacrifice has eternal consequences, having overcome the effects of sin for all times.

Third Reading (Mk 13:24-32): Mark evidently has Daniel in mind as he writes of Christ's sermon on the end of the world. Jesus uses the parable of the fig tree to point up His message. While the signs will be present, only God himself knows the exact day and hour for the destruction of the world.

Thought for the Day: The liturgy for today is concerned with God's plan for the world and its ultimate destruction as we know it. Jesus is warning us that we can lose all by failing to be on our watch and at prayer. Each of us will in all likelihood die the same way we live. We cannot expect a sudden and miraculous conversion. We must be ever on the ready to meet Jesus.

Feast of Christ the King   < B

Theme: It is fitting that the Church closes out the ecclesiastical year with the Feast of the Kingship of Christ. This kingdom is not a geographical area but is a kingdom of the spirit, found in the hearts of men.

First Reading (Dn 7:13-14): Daniel uses a term, son of man, which Christ will make His own. Daniel sees his king ruling over all peoples, for all time, by the power of the Father.

Responsorial Psalm (Ps 93): A hymn in praise of the heavenly king.

Second Reading (Rv 1:5-8): As he begins the Book of Revelation, St. John composes a hymn of praise to Jesus Christ, who won His kingship through His death, and who by redeeming us made us a royal nation in the service of the Father.

Third Reading (Jn 18:33-37): The famous scene where Christ declares His kingship before Pilate is recounted. Jesus is giving testimony to the Father before the world. This is His whole purpose of existence. Jesus explains this to Pilate, leaving him the option of a choice; Jesus forces no one.

Thought for the Day: The readings today offer a great contrast of the ways in which people react to Jesus. In the first two readings the king is looked upon in a spirit of faith and trust. Pilate approaches Jesus with worldly skepticism. The readings illustrate the choice each one of us has. We can approach Jesus in faith and remain with Him through His passion. On the other hand, we can hold ourselves aloof and refuse to comprehend His words. A great deal depends on which way we choose to go.

Year C

Nativity Cycle

First Sunday of Advent   < C

Theme: Advent is a season of hope, and Christmas is the promise of the accomplishment of that hope. The liturgy today is concerned with the Second Coming of Christ. St. Luke gives us the theme: Watch and pray.

First Reading (Jer 33:14-16): Although Jeremiah is often pictured as a prophet of gloom, he is in reality a prophet of great hope. We begin the new ecclesiastical and liturgical year with a reminder that God will raise up from the lineage of David "a just shoot" who will be Christ our Lord.

Responsorial Psalm (Ps 25): The spirit of Advent is exemplified in this psalm, which looks to God for salvation.

Second Reading (1 Thes 3:12 — 4:2): Paul looks to the Second Coming, but he is theologically mature enough to realize that this will not happen until all men have the opportunity to hear the Gospel and be saved. We should be constant and watchful because we know not the time and we should prepare ourselves, particularly by practicing charity.

Third Reading (Lk 21:25-28, 34-36): Our Lord gives a program for preparing for the end of the world: watchfulness and prayer. Because the end of history is hidden from us, this program is not something to be adopted hurriedly in the last days. It is one we are to live with daily.

Thought for the Day: If we look at the world around us,

there are many reasons to become discouraged. We live under the threat of a nuclear and universal holocaust. Yet even the most terrible things we can imagine will come to an end. The Second Coming of Christ offers us hope. This is what Advent is all about.

Second Sunday of Advent < C

Theme: This and next Sunday the Church turns our attention to John the Baptist, who prepared the way for Christ. He is held up as an example for our own preparation.

First Reading (Bar 5:1-9): Baruch appears very seldom in the liturgy. Today, however, the Church selects this prophet of the exile to speak of the final salvation that will come to Jerusalem. These words of Baruch are a commentary on the prophecy of Isaiah quoted by Luke in his Gospel. These words will find fulfillment in the New Jerusalem of Christ.

Responsorial Psalm (Ps 126): A hymn of joy for the returning exiles.

Second Reading (Phil 1:4-6, 8-11): His Philippian converts were always a joy to St. Paul, and this spirit is carried over in his letter to those who have promoted the Gospel teachings since the moment of their conversion. He reminds them that they must prepare to meet Christ on the day to come. This thought is also at the heart of Advent.

Third Reading (Lk 3:1-6): In this reading Luke sets the political and religious scene as it existed at the time of Jesus' coming. John has one purpose: to prepare the way for the Lord. John is but a prelude, for it is Jesus who will fulfill the promise of the Father.

Thought for the Day: We are always moving towards something. Many do not know the goal they seek and try to find it in the passing pleasures of the world. It was St. Augustine who told us that our hearts will always be restless until they find rest in God. Christians, following John's example, should make this fact known to all humanity.

Third Sunday of Advent   <   C

Theme: Joy in the Lord, the Lord who is coming.

First Reading (Zep 3:14-18): Zephaniah's prophecy of punishment speaks to the remnant of Israel. He concludes with this joyful psalm because Israel's salvation is at hand. His words foreshadow John the Baptist and fit well into the Advent theme.

Responsorial Psalm (Is 12:2-6): The Great One of Israel is in your midst.

Second Reading (Phil 4:4-7): This reading, which bids us to rejoice, gives this Sunday (Gaudete Sunday) its name. Our salvation is at hand, bringing a peace beyond understanding.

Third Reading (Lk 3:10-18): John the Baptist is the last prophet of the Old Testament, the bridge to the New. As the new covenant dawns, John calls for repentance. Unless we reject the old ways, we cannot receive the new life. John baptizes with water, but the baptism of Christ will be of the Spirit. John's challenge is to salvation or destruction.

Thought for the Day: We do not wait for the coming of the Lord in fear and trepidation, but with joy because we know that in Him is our salvation. Advent recalls the historical First Coming of Christ, and it is the promise of the Second Coming when all things will be made new. It is also a reminder that Jesus is among us now, in the Church and in His Body and Blood.

Fourth Sunday of Advent   <   C

Theme: Whether we are ready or not, the Church is. The liturgy focuses on Mary, who will make Christmas possible and on Bethlehem, the scene of Christ's birth.

First Reading (Mi 5:1-4): After the conquest of Canaan, the Ephrathah clan of the tribe of Judah settled in Bethlehem. It is from among these people the Savior will come. This is the clearest prophecy of the birthplace of Jesus.

Responsorial Psalm (Ps 80): A plea for God's help and a promise of constancy.

Second Reading (Heb 10:5-10): Jesus came on earth to do the will of his Father in heaven. In offering himself as our Savior, Jesus did away with the need of traditional sacrifices because He himself is the eternal sacrifice, made once and for all.

Third Reading (Lk 1:39-45): We are familiar with the story of the visitation — Mary's journey to Elizabeth, the Baptist's recognition of Christ, Elizabeth's salute to Mary's divine motherhood, and Mary's prophetic Magnificat. In this reading we see the operative hand of God in human destiny. Christmas is at hand, and God has taken on human life.

Thought for the Day: It is fitting that Advent should close with its focus on Mary. By her consent Christ is coming among us. She who has surrendered herself to the will of God now becomes the mother of humanity. The old world has ended and a new world begins.

Christmas: See Year A, pages 4-6.

Holy Family (Sunday in Octave of Christmas): See Year A, page 6.

Mary, Mother of god (Jan. 1): See Year A, page 7.

Epiphany (Sunday between Jan. 2-8): See Year A, page 8.

Baptism of the Lord (First Sunday of the Year, Sunday after Epiphany): See Year A, page 9.

Paschal Cycle

First Sunday of Lent   < C

Theme: There is a twofold theme on this First Sunday of Lent: resistance of temptation and the need of always making thanksgiving for what God has done for us.

First Reading (Dt 26:4-10): Exodus is never far from Jewish consciousness, hence their need always to render thanksgiving for their deliverance from Egyptian hands. Moses ordered them to return to God a sacrifice from the first fruits of the harvest.

Responsorial Psalm (Ps 91): A traditional prayer of confidence in God's care.

Second Reading (Rom 10:8-13): Paul sees faith in both an internal and external context. Belief is necessary for salvation, but that belief must be expressed in outward deeds — "By their fruit you shall know them."

Third Reading (Lk 4:1-13): Following His baptism, Jesus went into the wilderness to prepare for His mission. His forty-day retreat ends with a triple temptation: to use His powers for himself, to gain political power, to perform something spectacular that will make Him famous. Jesus dismisses the temptations because the Holy Spirit is guiding Him not to worldly conquest but to a road of suffering for our salvation.

Thought for the Day: In these days, when even sin itself is dismissed, the subject of temptations is seldom talked about. Yet the same temptations that assailed Christ are presented to each one of us in varying forms. Like Our Lord, we must recognize these temptations for what they are: means to draw us from the kingdom of God. Lent is a time when we gird ourselves so that we can more readily recognize and reject the temptations that subtly come to us from the paganism of the world in which we live.

Second Sunday of Lent   < C

Theme: God intervenes in human history in order to make known His will.

First Reading (Gn 15:5-12, 17-18): God makes His covenant with Abraham, rewarding his faith. God promises that out of Abraham he will form a great people who will not be entirely free of problems but over whom He will watch. Abraham seals the agreement with his sacrifices.

Responsorial Psalm (Ps 27): This psalm reflects Abraham's trust in God.

Second Reading (Phil 3:17-4:1): Paul exhorts his favorite Philippians to keep their trust in God. Their reward is in heaven, where they will be transfigured and glorified. He holds himself up as an example.

Third Reading (Lk 9:28-36): The Transfiguration comes at the end of Christ's Galilean ministry before He begins His journey to Jerusalem and His death. Although this mountain revelation was to strengthen the faith of Peter, John and James, it is also meant for all of us. Luke tells us that Moses and Elijah, each of whom had personal experience with God while alive, spoke with Jesus about what lay ahead in Jerusalem.

Thought for the Day: No other biblical figure displayed faith and trust in God as did Abraham. Not only did he uproot his family from a secure life, but he was prepared to sacrifice his only son for a God of whom he was just becoming aware. He was truly a man of faith. Our own faith benefits from a long series of revelations, including the Transfiguration. This faith, when meditated upon, should increase our commitment to Christ.

Third Sunday of Lent   < C

Theme: The liturgy today calls upon us to reform and change our lives. The Church gives us an example from the Old and New Testaments.

First Reading (Ex 3:1-8, 13-15): Moses receives his calling from God in a dramatic way, during which God gives his name, "I AM." Like Abraham in last week's liturgy, Moses has direct contact with God. He leaves his flocks and father-in-law to do God's work with Israel. His response is immediate and complete.

Responsorial Psalm (Ps 103): A hymn of thanksgiving to God, who, as the psalm says, "made known his ways to Moses," referring to the first reading.

Second Reading (1 Cor 10:1-6, 10-12): Paul warns his new Christians about overconfidence. He reminds them of the many blessings God gave the Israelites in the desert, yet many were destroyed by God for lack of faith. This should be a warning that anyone can fall.

Third Reading (Lk 13:1-9): As Jesus moves on to Jerusalem, He begins to warn His hearers of the danger in failing to repent. In the Gospel today, He takes two current happenings of tragedies and warns that even greater dangers await those who do not accept the reformation He offers.

Thought for the Day: Lent is the time for us to ask ourselves hard questions. While it is a period for us to do penance, it is more than mere giving up of things. We empty ourselves so that we might be filled. What we need to be filled with is Christ. Lent is a time for turning back to God. It is a challenge for us to be converted.

Fourth Sunday of Lent   < C

Theme: Reconciliation with God.

First Reading (Jos 5:9-12): Joshua, successor to Moses, led the Israelites into the Promised Land, crossing the Jordan, whose waters were held back as in the passage through the Red Sea. On the plain of Jericho the people celebrated the Passover and the rain of the miraculous manna ended. From now on their food would be from the earth. The liberation of the Israelites has been accomplished.

Responsorial Psalm (Ps 34): A reminder that God cares for and feeds His people.

Second Reading (2 Cor 5:17-21): Christ's primary task was reconciling humanity with the Father. St. Paul reminds the Corinthians that Jesus has "entrusted the message of reconciliation to us." We must reconcile ourselves with the Father and become ambassadors for Christ.

Third Reading (Lk 15:1-3, 11-32): We are familiar with the story of the prodigal son. There are two meanings to this parable. One is the reconciliation of those who have abandoned God. The second is that the two sons represent the Jewish and Gentile worlds. The Jews should not complain that God welcomes their brothers into one family.

Thought for the Day: The world today badly needs reconciliation with the Father. The daily headlines tell of our alienation from God and its results: suicides, abortions, murders, international intrigues, loss of family life, pornography, the mad quest for happiness in drugs. People serve their own desires and not God's.

Fifth Sunday of Lent   < C

Theme: While at first today's readings seem disjointed, careful examination produces a theme: Forget the past, begin anew.

First Reading (Is 43:16-21): Second Isaiah is marked by looking toward the future. His message today is not to consider the events of long ago but to look to the new exodus which God is forming.

Responsorial Psalm (Ps 126): When the Jews returned to Zion from captivity, they were like new people, unable to comprehend that life had been restored to them again.

Second Reading (Phil 3:8-14): Nothing really matters in life but Christ. Paul has given up everything for his Faith. However, conversion is only the beginning point; one still has the whole race to run. For Paul, his attention is on the finish line and its eternal prize — life with Christ.

Third Reading (Jn 8:1-11): Jesus did not worry about what the woman taken in adultery did in the past but what she would do in the future. He will not condemn her if she will avoid future sin. Those who had condemned her walked away and did not receive His reconciliation. Jesus calls for repentance, and the woman responds. (Another Gospel can be read today from Year A. It concerns the resurrection of Lazarus and its foreshadowing of our own resurrection.)

Thought for the Day: We hear so much today of people seeking "meaning" in life. Paul found that meaning in Christ and the power flowing from His resurrection. To find Christ means to repent the past and begin new life — in short, a total conversion.

Passion (Palm) Sunday: See Year A, pages 14-15.

Easter Sunday: See Year A, page 15.

Second Sunday of Easter   < C

Theme: The risen Lord gave the Holy Spirit to the Church. As members of the Church we share in the same Spirit and its powers.

First Reading (Acts 5:12-16): St. Luke, author of Acts, traces the development of the new Church under the guidance of the Holy Spirit. In this reading he tells of the growth of the Church in Jerusalem under Peter and the other apostles, who continue the healing work and miracles of Jesus.

Responsorial Psalm (Ps 118): An Easter hymn of thanks to God.

Second Reading (Rv 1:9-11, 12-13, 17-19): John begins the revelations that came to him when he was exiled on Patmos. Through the power of the Spirit, John is taken out of this world to view the heavenly kingdom and its mysteries, of which the risen Christ is the center. He is commanded to write down his visions in what is the most difficult of all scriptural books to interpret.

Third Reading (Jn 20:19-31): Most commentators of this account of Christ's first appearance to His apostles dwell on the doubt of Thomas and the necessity of faith. However, the real heart is in the establishment of the Sacrament of Penance and Christ's gift of the Holy Spirit. John ends his Gospel satisfied that he has proven Christ to be the Messiah.

Thought for the Day: Vatican II referred to the Church as "the universal sacrament of salvation." The Father sent the Son into the world to redeem it. Now returned to the Father, the Son sends the Holy Spirit to guide the Church for all time and to work in a particular way through its priests.

Third Sunday of Easter   <   C

Theme: Just as the mission of the Church met with opposition in its infancy, so too was it opposed even down to our own times. Like the apostles, our hope is in the risen Lord, in whom we can expect ultimate victory.

First Reading (Acts 5:27-32, 40-41): The Jewish leaders warn Peter and the apostles not to preach Jesus because they are disturbed that the movement is attracting too many people. Their opposition will result in the death of Stephen. Peter replies boldly that they are obeying God. Despite the warnings, he and his companions leave the Sanhedrin happily.

Responsorial Psalm (Ps 30): A stirring song of complete

confidence that God delivers His followers from their enemies.

Second Reading (Rv 5:11-14): John continues his heavenly vision. The risen Christ is triumphant and worthy of all praise. As the slain Lamb, He is the sole mediator between God's throne and all angels and people.

Third Reading (Jn 21:1-19): There is much symbolism in this post-resurrection account of Christ meeting with His apostles. Peter, who had denied Christ three times is now given an equal number of chances to profess his love. Christ charges the head of the Church to feed His flock with His truth. The teeming fishing net indicates the great number who will enter the Church. Finally, Peter's death by martyrdom in imitation of the Master is foretold.

Thought for the Day: As disciples, the question asked of Peter is also asked of us. Do we really love Jesus?

Fourth Sunday of Easter   < C

Theme: Today is Good Shepherd Sunday, and while the accent of the liturgy is on Christ, the Good Shepherd, we are reminded that we are "his people, the flock he tends."

First Reading (Acts 13:14, 43-52): We have been following the development of the Church as recorded in Acts. The Faith has been preached in Jerusalem and then throughout Palestine. Now the missionary journeys of Paul and Barnabas take the new religion to non-Jews. Here, Acts outlines the pattern Paul will follow in his missionary work: first, preaching to Jews; when they reject the message, turning to the Gentiles, who respond with delight. Paul's persecution by his fellow Jews will follow him throughout his apostolate.

Responsorial Psalm (Ps 100): A hymn of praise to God because we are "his people, the flock he tends."

Second Reading (Rv 7:9, 14-17): John continues his vision of heaven, which he finds difficult to describe in words. Here he portrays those who have suffered the trials and tribulations of the world but have remained in the flock of Christ. It is significant that the saved include people of all tribes and nations, again emphasizing that Christianity belongs to all men.

Third Reading (Jn 10:27-30): Today's reading concludes

Jesus' sermon on the Good Shepherd. Here He places emphasis on His flock, giving assurance that those who belong to it will never be lost. This theme is introduced into the liturgy at this time because it is by His death for His sheep that He truly becomes the Good Shepherd. We are His sheep because He purchased us with His life.

Thought for the Day: The shepherd spends his life with his flock, guarding it and caring for its needs. Jesus uses this close relationship to bring out two points: His own relationship with the Father, and His relationship with us. Jesus is a model for our relationship with all our own brothers and sisters of the world.

Fifth Sunday of Easter   < C

Theme: The Easter readings continue the theme of the new creation. They are meant to give us strength, courage and guidance. Today's Gospel depicts the identifying mark of the new Church: "Love one another as I have loved you."

First Reading (Acts 14:21-27): Last week we read of Paul and Barnabas beginning their missionary journeys after being commissioned by the Holy Spirit in Antioch. Today they return to that city to report to the brethren what they have accomplished, particularly among the Gentiles. Their success was to lead to the first council of the Church, that of Jerusalem.

Responsorial Psalm (Ps 145): A hymn of praise to God, king of all.

Second Reading (Rv 21:1-5): John explains the new creation in terms of his vision of the new Jerusalem, where evil has been destroyed and pain and sorrow no longer exist. The Resurrection began the work of this new creation, and John sees its fulfillment when the fruits of the triumphant Christ come upon mankind.

Third Reading (Jn 13:31-35): After Judas has left, Jesus starts his great discourse at the Last Supper. He begins speaking enigmatically, so much so, that shortly Philip and Jude will interrupt the sermon to question Him. The hour for His sacrifice is at hand, and He must leave his apostles. With His death He is establishing a new structure for the world, one based on love, reflecting the love He has for His Church. This love will be the way that His followers may be identified.

Thought for the day: Without Jesus revealing the love of the Father, there would be no meaning to life or to the world. There can be no hope, no sanity, no true freedom. If we are true Christians, we will love everyone with the love of Christ. Only that can give meaning to life.

Sixth Sunday of Easter < C

Theme: The Holy Spirit is emphasized in this Sunday's liturgy. Not only does He guide the early Church but is Christ's special gift to His followers.

First Reading (Acts 15:1-2, 22-29). Almost two decades after the first preaching of the Gospel began there were still disputes over the manner in which it should be presented to the Gentiles. There were some who wanted to Judaize these new Christians. Paul and Barnabas went to Jerusalem. Some argued that the law of Moses should be followed in its entirety. The conclusion of the apostles and elders of the Church, however, was that "It is the decision of the Holy Spirit, and ours too," that the heavy ritualistic burden of Judaism should not be placed on converts from paganism.

Responsorial Psalm (Ps 67): With the Gospel being preached to the nations, all peoples everywhere can praise God.

Second Reading (Rv 21:10-14, 22-23): John sees the Church as the heavenly Jerusalem, entry into which is won by the faith taught by the Twelve Apostles, the foundations of the New Jerusalem.

Third Reading (Jn 14:23-29): Christ's last discourse is continued. His followers will keep His commandments, and God will dwell in them. The Holy Spirit will enlighten and guide those who believe in Him. Jesus' final gift is one of peace, a gift that will be sorely needed in the agonies that lie ahead.

Thought for the Day: The Holy Spirit is still with the Church, guarding it and guiding it. Men may fail Christ, but the Church will be ever faithful because its life is that of the Spirit.

Seventh Sunday of Easter < C

Theme: As we prepare for the great Feast of Pentecost, the Holy Spirit is still the theme of the liturgy. The Church finds it necessary to emphasize the importance of the Spirit in its own life and that of every Christian.

First Reading (Acts 7:55-60): Christ had promised that in times of persecution the Holy Spirit would guide the Christian in his acts and words. Today this promise is realized in Stephen, the first martyr. It is the Holy Spirit who puts the words into Stephen's mouth. It is the Holy Spirit who first touches the heart of Saul, who witnessed the execution — although at this time Saul does not realize this fact.

Responsorial Psalm (Ps 97): By the death of Stephen the heavens are open to reveal God's glory. Thus this hymn of praise is sung.

Second Reading (Rv 22:12-14, 16-17, 20): John hears Christ speak of the Second Coming. Jesus is the beginning and the end, the gate by which all must enter heaven. John closes his vision with the exclamation and prayer: "Come, Lord Jesus!"

Third Reading (Jn 17:20-26): Jesus is coming to the end of His last discourse, and He now prays for all those of all times who will believe in Him. He prays that they will have the same unity as He and the Father. But, alas, today we see the Body of Christ divided into many parts and the unity He prayed for far from accomplishment.

Thought for the Day: Everyone today talks about the need for unity, but the only true unity is to be found in the Church of Christ, where all celebrate one sacrifice and are moved by the one Spirit. We must work to make all peoples members of Christ's true Church.

Trinity Sunday < C

Theme: The Holy Trinity reveals the inmost life of God. It is a mystery which we can never fully comprehend no matter our wisdom. An equally great mystery is why God chooses to share His life with us, His creatures. This gift is out of love and teaches that we too must share our love with all creation.

First Reading (Prv 8:22-31): The poetic and inspired writer of this book ends his long praise of wisdom by telling us it is God's greatest gift to us. Wisdom is knowledge of what is essential in human life. It is the judgment we make of earthly treasures in the light of eternity. St. Thomas Aquinas tells us the wise man orders all things. The most important order for us is our relationship with eternal life. The Holy Trinity is true order.

Responsorial Psalm (Ps 9): A hymn of praise for creation and thanks that God has given us domination over His gifts.

Second Reading (Rom 5:1-5): In the person of faith, the Holy Trinity is at work. Jesus has made our peace with His Father. With the Father and Son within us, the gifts of the Holy Spirit make us spiritually rich.

Third Reading (Jn 16:12-15): In His last discourse, Jesus promises His disciples the gift of the Holy Spirit. This gift will involve the disciples in the innermost life of God, and the enlightenment given by the Spirit will enable them to preach it to all on earth.

Thought for the Day: In its document on *The Church in the Modern World*, Vatican II likens the union that exists between the three Divine Persons to the unity that should exist between God's children. Loving is expressed in giving. If we love God, we give ourselves to Him. This is a gift we must make daily to God and neighbor.

Corpus Christi   < C

Theme: The Feast of the Body and Blood of Christ commemorates His great miracle of His continued physical presence among us in the Eucharist. We resolve to receive Him often in Communion.

First Reading (Gn 14:18-20): As Eucharistic Prayer I reminds us, the priest Melchizedek offered bread and wine to God in behalf of Abraham, a prefigurement of Christ, just as his offering prefigured the Eucharist. These verses from Genesis are another insight into God's eternal plan of preparing for that which was to come to a climax at the Last Supper and on Calvary.

Responsorial Psalm (Ps 110): The Responsorial Psalm continues this theme, praising a Messiah, begotten by God, who will be forever a priest.

Second Reading (1 Cor 11:23-26): The Church repeats Paul's teaching that was used on Holy Thursday. The apostle to the Gentiles summarizes the history of the giving of the Eucharist, reminding the Corinthians that in partaking of the sacrament they unite themselves to Christ's eternal and continuing sacrifice.

Third Reading (Lk 9:11-17): The Church recounts one of the miracles Christ used to prepare His followers for the doctrine of the Eucharist, which He was shortly to reveal to them. Words from the Gospel are incorporated in the Rite of Consecration at the Mass. What Christ was saying in effect was: "See, if I can multiply this little bit of food to feed so many, do not be surprised when I tell you I can multiply myself to feed you of my own body and blood."

Thought for the Day: It is at the banquet of the Lord that His faithful gather to partake of His very life. This is no mere commemoration or symbol, but the actual taking of God within us. By Communion we are united physically to every other Catholic who receives Christ. Our resolution: never a Mass without Communion.

Ordinary Time

Second Sunday of the Year   < C

Theme: The relationship between God and His people is so intimate that it is best described in terms of an ideal marriage.

First Reading (Is 62:1-5): The Bible, by showing us the deep feeling the Jews had for Jerusalem, the center and hope of their lives, gives us a deep insight into how the Jews look upon today's Israel. Jerusalem was a symbol of their identity with God. Isaiah likens Jerusalem to a bride of Yahweh on whom He will bestow His richest gifts.

Responsorial Psalm (Ps 96): A song written by King David which was sung when he brought the Ark of the Covenant to Jerusalem, a reminder of God's eternal pact with humanity.

Second Reading (1 Cor 12:4-11): God gives many gifts to His people in many different ways, but they all have one purpose: God's glory. These gifts are not to be used for personal advancement but for the common good. Since they are gifts, they must be received humbly.

Third Reading (Jn 2:1-2): The miracle at the Wedding Feast of Cana comes at the beginning of the public life of Jesus. He has been baptized by John and has gathered the first half dozen of His apostles. At Cana not only does Christ sanctify marriage by His presence, but the occasion becomes a sign of His own intimacy with the Church.

Thought for the Day: Today the Sacrament of Marriage is under attack. People openly boast of living together outside of matrimony and state their fears of lasting relationships. The union of husband and wife is not a casual relationship, but it takes on the grandeur of God's own love for His people and the mystical union of the Church with Christ.

Third Sunday of the Year   < C

Theme: God's Word must be the object of belief, but belief is sterile unless it is obeyed. The law is not an instrument to crush the spirit but a promise of hope and rejoicing.

First Reading (Neh 8:2-6, 8-10): Although the Jews had returned to Israel from Babylonian exile, they were leaderless and uninstructed. Then Ezra came from Babylon to teach God's law. The people are so moved that they weep when God's law is read to them. Ezra tells them that it is a time for rejoicing.

Responsorial Psalm (Ps 19): The law of God is spirit and life.

Second Reading (1 Cor 12:12-30): In this beautiful and powerful passage, Paul stresses the unity of Christians. He outlines the unique Pauline teaching of the doctrine of the Mystical Body, of the Christian's essential union with the Church and Christ.

Third Reading (Lk 1:1-4, 4:14-21): Luke states the authenticity of his Gospel, in which he will prove the divinity and messiahship of Jesus. This Gospel tells of the beginning of Christ's Galilean ministry when he appears in the synagogue at Nazareth and uses the prophet Isaiah to establish His credentials. Immediately the people turn against Him and seek to put Him to death, but Jesus had foreseen this and predicted: "A prophet is never welcomed in his own country."

Thought for the Day: Listening to the Word of God is not mere hearing. It requires action. It also demands the abolishment of preconceived ideas. "Be doers of the word," Jesus told us. Only when the Word of God becomes active will the problems of the world find solution.

Fourth Sunday of the Year < C

Theme: God protects His prophets. He gives them always the strength to prevail. Just as He delivered Jeremiah from his enemies, so too he saved His Son from those who would kill Him.

First Reading (Jer 1:4-5, 17-19): Jeremiah preached his message that Yahweh is sole God, Lord of Creation and Master of History, at a time when the then known world was in turmoil as Assyria and Babylonia fought for control. Jeremiah sought to root out pagan practices, foreseeing the enslavement of Israel. In this reading, he states his vocation and assurance of God's blessing on his work.

Responsorial Psalm (Ps 71): Although a song of pain, the psalm is also one of trust. It reflects Jeremiah's life.

Second Reading (1 Cor 12:31 — 13:13): Here is St. Paul's classic and popular description of love (charity). Speaking to a Christian community torn by rivalries, Paul rises to the heights in outlining what its spirit should be.

Third Reading (Lk 4:21-30): This is a continuation of last week's Gospel. Christ declares His credentials to the people of Galilee and they reject Him. There is a foreshadowing here that God's teachings will now pass beyond Israel itself.

Thought for the Day: Love is probably the most abused word in the English language today. It has been prostituted in literature and by the commercial media. For millions the word has become synonymous with the sex act. Paul tells us of the necessity of love and then describes it for us. It is a descrip-

109

tion for the Christian to measure himself or herself against.

Fifth Sunday of the Year   < C

Theme: Just as Christ called His disciples, so He calls each one of us to His service. This is our Christian vocation.

First Reading (Is 6:1-8): Isaiah, like other prophets, recounts his own calling to the service of the Lord. He is compelled to give the incidents of his vision so that his credentials as a prophet of God's sanctity may be established. Of interest to us is his wholehearted response to the invitation of the Lord: "Here I am, send me!"

Responsorial Psalm (Ps 138): A temple chant of thanksgiving.

Second Reading (1 Cor 15:1-11): Paul is having a problem with some of his converts in Corinth who are finding a difficulty in accepting the resurrection of Christ. He begins his argument in defense of the resurrection by appealing to witnesses and tradition. He tells them that many people are still alive who saw the resurrected Christ.

Third Reading (Lk 5:1-11): Jesus began his public mission from a base at Capernaum on Lake Galilee. He has been rejected in Nazareth and now symbolically begins His mission to the world. The first task is to build the structure of His future Church, and for this He needs help. Now He enlists Peter, James and John and promises Peter that in place of fish, he shall henceforth catch men. Peter's response is the same as Isaiah's. He leaves all and follows Jesus.

Thought for the Day: God does His work through men and women, the ordinary means of salvation. In baptism we were consecrated to the service of Christ, and this vocation was renewed in Confirmation. The salvation of many can depend upon our efforts.

Sixth Sunday of the Year   < C

Theme: The Church today gives us some rules for living.

First Reading (Jer 17:5-8): For Jeremiah one should place his confidence only in God and not in worldly powers. The man or woman who does not is barren. The person who trusts in God is like a tree with an abundant water supply. For Jeremiah this is a matter of growth in God.

Responsorial Psalm (Ps 1): This psalm continues the imagery of Jeremiah.

Second Reading (1 Cor 15:12, 16-20): Paul continues his discourse on the Resurrection. He makes the Resurrection the keystone to faith. If Christ was not resurrected, then faith is in vain. The fact is that Christ did rise from the dead, and in that is the promise of our own resurrection.

Third Reading (Lk 6:17, 20-26): In this discourse of Christ, Luke parallels the Sermon on the Mount of Matthew and for his purpose lists only four of the nine beatitudes and accompanies these with four woes. Those who follow Jesus will be outcasts who will be reviled and insulted. This, however, is no reason for sorrow but for rejoicing. The ones who really are to be pitied are the rich and content, happy now, but in great danger of losing salvation.

Thought for the Day: How true is today's Gospel! We live in times of prosperity and comfort never imagined by our ancestors. While prosperity in itself is not wrong because it makes available a greater portion of God's creation for His uses, selfish use is wrong. How can we justify the enormous sums spent for beauty aids and other foolish luxuries when millions are starving? This Gospel should raise practical questions for us and our habits.

Seventh Sunday of the Year   < C

Theme: Love your enemies; do good to those who hate you.

First Reading (1 Sm 26): Saul is intent on hunting down and killing David. At night David enters his enemy's camp and stands over the sleeping Saul. He refuses to harm the king, whom he recognizes as the Lord's anointed, thus proving himself faithful to God and the king.

Responsorial Psalm (Ps 103): A reminder that God is merciful. Out of love He forgives our most serious sins. Can we do less to others?

Second Reading (1 Cor 15:35-49): The Corinthians have been asking Paul about their own resurrection. How will they be raised from the dead? What kind of bodies will they have? Paul says that these are foolish questions. Christ has proved by His resurrection that we will be raised again to a spiritual existence. He contrasts Adam and Christ. Through Adam we became living souls. Through Christ we become eternal spirits.

Third Reading (Lk 6:27-38): Christ's teaching on charity is very radical. We do not love merely those who are good to us but those who would harm us. We render good for evil. We give without expecting repayment. God will judge us as we judge others. He will measure out to us by the same yardstick we use in our relations with others. This is an essential and basic Christian doctrine.

Thought for the Day: The liturgy today clearly shows that we are called upon to rise above the natural and lead a supernatural life. By nature we resent offenders, the stupid, those who oppose us. Christian charity, however, tells us that we must love all these people, that we are to do good without expecting any return. Our reward will come from God and not from men or women.

Eighth Sunday of the Year < C

Theme: We reveal ourselves by our actions, particularly by our speech. Both Ben Sira and Jesus advise us that words reveal the character of the person.

First Reading (Sir 27:4-7): "Do not praise a man before he has spoken," Ben Sira (Ecclesiasticus) advises his readers. The defects of a person appear in his or her speech. A person may try to disguise true character, but sufficient speech will reveal it.

Responsorial Psalm (Ps 92): The just person will give thanks to the Lord and because of this will flourish.

Second Reading (1 Cor 15:45-58): Death is not the end for the Christian. Victory comes in the immortality of resurrection. Only sin can bring about a victory for death.

Third Reading (Lk 6:39-45): Jesus could be giving a homily on Ben Sira's advice. A person is good because of what is in the heart, and these dispositions are revealed by actions, particularly through speech. A person's words flow from what fills the heart.

Thought for the Day: How often do we speak an unkind word or give a twist to the truth! Such words say something about ourselves, that there is something within us that should not be there. We should listen to ourselves and learn.

Ninth Sunday of the Year   < C

Theme: God is the Father of all peoples, everywhere. The religion His Son founded is open to people of every race and tribe. All are called to be members of His kingdom.

First Reading (1 Kgs 8:41-43): Solomon built the first great temple to Yahweh, finishing it about a thousand years before the birth of Christ. At the dedication of this magnificent structure, Solomon declared that it would be open to all peoples as long as they came to pray to the Lord.

Responsorial Psalm (Ps 117): All peoples of the world are urged to praise the One God.

Second Reading (Gal 1:1-2, 6-10): This is the opening of Paul's letter to the Church in Galatia, a region now in southern Turkey to which Paul came on his first missionary journey. Paul is angry that Judeo-Christians have negated his teachings, and there is a reproving tone to this introduction to the epistle.

Third Reading (Lk 7:1-10): This is the familiar story of the healing of the Roman officer's servant. It shows the belief of non-Jews in Jesus, but also depicts the great faith in and understanding of Jesus that the centurion possessed.

Thought for the Day: Because of Israel's covenant with God, Jesus first offered the New Covenant to the Jewish people. Many of them did accept His teaching, but the Jewish establishment turned a deaf ear. As the Gospels develop, Jesus more and more opens His teachings to all because it was for all that they are ultimately intended. Are we concerned with and active in the preaching of the Gospel to those who do not know Jesus?

Tenth Sunday of the Year   < C

Theme: Compassion means "to feel with." The compassion

of Jesus went out to the poor, sick and needy with whom He identified. In today's readings life is restored to two sons, once by a compassionate Elijah and again by a compassionate Christ.

First Reading (1 Kgs 17:17-24): In Jewish tradition great compassion was shown to widows. There was no social security in those days, and widows depended on the charity of neighbors. Hence the loss of an only child was a grave loss. In this incident, which prefigures Christ's own miracle, Elijah raises a dead son to life.

Responsorial Psalm (Ps 30): God raises us from the dead.

Second Reading (Gal 1:11-19): This is a continuation of last Sunday's reading. Paul states his credentials to the Galatians: from persecutor to apostle because he was called by God himself.

Third Reading (Lk 7:11-17): The only son of the widow of Nain is brought back to life by Jesus in an act which astounds the people. They recognize the hand of God is here.

Thought for the Day: While the miracle at Nain shows the power of Jesus and proves His claim to be Son of God, it also shows the compassion Jesus has for us in our needs. When one of us suffers, all in the Mystical Body suffer. We must identify ourselves with our needy brothers and sisters if we are to be true Christians.

Eleventh Sunday of the Year   < C

Theme: God's forgiveness of sin. David and the sinful woman are far apart in time, history and importance, but both find forgiveness through repentance and the desire to be forgiven.

First Reading (2 Sm 12:7-10, 13): Everything David had, he owed to God. Despite this he failed God miserably, committing adultery with the wife of a foreign soldier and then having the man killed in battle. When David repents, Nathan pronounces his forgiveness. From the sin comes Solomon, David's successor and ancestor of Jesus. Yet sin is not without its effects. From David's sin also will come fratricidal hatred and murder.

Responsorial Psalm (Ps 63): David's song: Happy is the man whose offense is forgiven.

Second Reading (Gal 2:16, 19-21: Faith in Jesus Christ is the way to salvation, and the Old Law no longer suffices. Then Paul tells us what a Christian is: one who lives the life of Christ. Unless we live a life of faith, we have no benefits from the sacrifice of Christ.

Third Reading (Lk 7:36 — 8:3): This follows immediately after the reading of why Jesus is not like John the Baptist, penitential and a hermit. In this incident in Simon's house, Jesus shows why He has come on earth: to call sinners to repentance and to heal them with His love. We too might ask with those invited guests, "Who is this man, that he even forgives sin?"

Thought for the Day: Christ's mission was one of healing, not so much the body, which He did dramatically only to show His total power, but to heal the very soul of a person. He accomplished this by reconciling us to God. All He asked were sorrow and atonement. The Church continues to this day the reconciling mission of Christ.

Twelfth Sunday of the Year   < C

Theme: The thought of the crucified Christ is never far from the heart of the liturgy. Through the merits of the Cross, all people are enabled to become one in Christ because of their recognition of Him as the Messiah.

First Reading (Zec 12:10-11): Zechariah presents us with a messianic prophecy. From the house of David shall come the Messiah, who shall be put to death. Many Jews will realize what has been done is an injustice and shall mourn their deed.

Responsorial Psalm (Ps 63): Just as Zechariah and the other prophets longed for the Messiah, so too does the psalmist, who while waiting for the prophecies to be fulfilled expresses his confidence in God.

Second Reading (Gal 3:26-29): The Messiah, Jesus Christ, makes all sisters and brothers, children of a common heavenly Father, co-heirs of the kingdom of heaven.

Third Reading (Lk 9:18-24): Peter proclaims Christ to be the Messiah. In order that His apostles might not misunderstand and expect a worldly king, however, Jesus foretells His death and resurrection. He preaches the great paradox of Christianity, that to save our life we must lose it by dying to self and serving only Him.

Thought for the Day: The liturgy today reveals the true mission of Christ: to die for us. We cannot escape suffering in our own lives, so as Christians we should merit from our sufferings by uniting them with those of our Savior.

Thirteenth Sunday of the Year < C

Theme: The heart of today's liturgical message is following Christ in complete abandonment to personal preferences. If we follow the teaching of Christ, our way to God will be the way of love, even disregarding our own needs in favor of those of another.

First Reading (1 Kgs 19:16, 19-21): Elisha left family and flocks to follow the prophet Elijah. His action foreshadows the apostles, who will leave their homes, families and businesses to follow Christ. How many obstacles do we put in the way of following the Master!

Responsorial Psalm (Ps 16): This is a song of the promises of God if we follow His will and abandon ourselves to Him.

Second Reading (Gal 5:1, 13-18): Paul extols freedom. His freedom is not license but liberty in doing God's will. One of the primary desires of that will is that we should love one another. The Christian community that is torn by jealousies and disputes and personal preferences will come to ruin. The community that lives in God's spirit will find peace and love.

Third Reading (Lk 9:51-62): Luke begins his long account of Christ's final journey to Jerusalem. As he describes the words and deeds of Jesus, he has in mind the prophet Elijah, who refused to destroy his enemies and who demanded total commitment to God. Christ demands this same commitment from His followers; they are not to look back at what they left but follow Him in complete trust. This is a crucial Gospel because it gives the signs by which the true follower of Christ can be known.

Thought for the Day: How far am I willing to go for Christ? Could I give up the things I love the most? Do I really try to make Christ's life my own? Am I ready to love those who do not like me? In short, am I really a Christian?

Fourteenth Sunday of the Year   < C

Theme: The Church of Christ is the New Jerusalem of which the prophets foretold. We are to spread that Church.

First Reading (Is 66:10-14): The Book of Isaiah fittingly closes with the prophet singing the praises of the New Jerusalem which is to come. When that day arrives the people of God will be comforted and will rejoice in the Lord's power. We know now that what the prophet was referring to was the reign of Christ, the true new Jerusalem.

Responsorial Psalm (Ps 66): A hymn of praise and thanks to God for hearing the prayer of mankind.

Second Reading (Gal 6:14-18): As it did in the first reading, the Church chooses final summary verses this time from St. Paul's letter to the Galatians, in which he presents a concise statement of his teachings, the proof of which are the marks of Christ he bears on his own body. The Old Law has ended and no longer binds since Christ has built a new world, which all of God's people are invited to join.

Third Reading (Lk 10:1-12, 17-20): The Gospel today is given in a long and short form, both of which tell of the commissioning of His disciples to go out in groups, preparing His way by preaching His message. Preaching the Gospel is not an easy task because we must depart from the values of the world and devote ourselves completely and confidently to God.

Thought for the Day: St. Paul tells us that God wishes all people to be saved. Therefore, the missionary nature of the Church is of its very essence. It is a work in which everyone of us must take some part, either actively or through support. What am I doing in a positive way to make Christ known? Am I ready to disregard the scorn of the world for my beliefs in Christ?

Fifteenth Sunday of the Year   < C

Theme: The name of our neighbor is everyman, but only because we are part of Christ, who is all in all, without beginning or end.

First Reading (Dt 30:10-14): Moses, in his last sermon,

dwells on the word of God as always present to His people. That word is not far distant from us, but alive and active in each one's conscience.

Responsorial Psalm (Ps 69): A prayer for help in time of need, and the promise that the Lord hears His own.

Second Reading (Col 1:15-20): In one of his most poetic and beautiful descriptions of Jesus, Paul summarizes his beliefs in Christ for the Colossians, some of whom saw Jesus as only one mediator among many. Paul tells us that Jesus is the head of the Church, the one in whom all creation has its being. Jesus is the beginning and the end, without whom life would have no meaning.

Third Reading (Lk 10:25-37): The parable of the Good Samaritan is a familiar one to us. Jesus not only tells us that we must consider every person on earth our neighbor but that the law of God means nothing unless we practice it. The Samaritan understood the meaning of the law better than those who were skilled in its intricacies.

Thought for the Day: Jesus told us that not every man who says, "Lord, Lord!" will enter the kingdom of heaven but he who does the will of His Father. And the Father's will is that we love everyone on earth. It may be easy to give lip service to this commandment for those at a distance, but what is our reaction to the person next door, the one who cuts in front of us in traffic, the one who tells others ill about us? They are all our neighbors. Do we react to them as followers of Christ or from our own personal inclinations?

Sixteenth Sunday of the Year   < C

Theme: Love of neighbor, love of God.

First Reading (Gn 18:1-10): God appears to us in many forms. In today's account from Genesis, He appears in the guise of strangers. Abraham receives them without question, serves them his finest food. They know all about him and his childless wife. Then they make to him a promise that only God could make: Before the year is out Sarah will bear Abraham the long-desired son. Abraham exhibits true love of neighbor and his reward is great.

Responsorial Psalm (Ps 15): He who does justice will find God. What is justice? Love of God and neighbor.

Second Reading (Col 1:24-28): Christ died that the Good News might be given to all men. Paul is now driven to give that News to all who lack it. Paul's example truly exhibits his love of God and neighbor, for what greater gift can he give others than news of salvation?

Third Reading (Lk 10:38-42): Today's Gospel has many interpretations. It is used as an argument for contemplation. Others say that it shows we should avoid the cares of the world. The simplest interpretation is that of the theme of this liturgy. Mary represents the true follower of God who is intent on God's love; she pays attention to Jesus, her neighbor and God. Martha might represent those who become so involved in the cares of everyday living or those concerns of the law that they forget the essential thing: Jesus himself is here and must be served by being in His presence. Nothing else matters.

Thought for the Day: How many excuses do I make in failing to serve God and my neighbor? I excuse myself from opportunities offered by the Church because I am busy at home or have something else to do. My neighbor is everyman and he cries to me continually for help. My ear is deaf to his hunger, his miseries, his everyday wants. How will I respond to God in judgment when he puts me to this test? (Mt 25:31-46)

Seventeenth Sunday of the Year   < C

Theme: The liturgy today reminds us of the closeness we can have with God and the confidence we can place in His hearing our prayer.

First Reading (Gn 18:20-32): There are many lessons to be drawn from this reading. The intimacy that existed between God and Adam, with whom He also walked, is now shown between God and Abraham, in many ways the successor of Adam. So close is Abraham to God that he can argue with the Father about sparing the wicked cities of Sodom and Gomorrah.

Responsorial Psalm (Ps 138): The Lord hears our prayers and will help us.

Second Reading (Col 2:12-14): Paul writes against the background of Jewish Christians trying to Judaize the Colossians. He tells them that when they were reborn in baptism, they had no need of Jewish law. When Christ rose from the dead, all who have been baptized rose with Him into new life without attachments to the old.

Third Reading (Lk 11:1-3): The apostles realize that they cannot be successful in their work without a spirit of prayer, and so they ask Christ to teach them to pray. He gives them the perfect prayer, the Our Father. In it we pray not only for our daily material needs but for the Bread of Life, the Eucharist. Jesus tells us to ask the Father for what we need, promising that every prayer will be answered.

Thought for the Day: Prayer is at the heart of today's liturgical message. There are two types of prayer. The first and foremost is the community prayer which we attend in the Eucharist. It is offered in the name of all the people of God. It has little meaning, however, unless it is carried over into our own personal lives. Abraham gives us the example of how we should pray: intimately and confidently. This second type, personal prayer, must never be far from our hearts.

Eighteenth Sunday of the Year   <   C

Theme: Would that we had the wisdom to judge the value of things the way God does! All that the world esteems — power and wealth — is an empty boast in God's value system.

First Reading (Eccl 1:2; 2:21-23): Vanity is an inordinate love for the esteem of others. Ecclesiastes, the preacher, tells us that most of our actions spring from vanity. He anticipates Christ's question: "What profit does a man show who gains the whole world and destroys himself in the process?" (Mk 8:36)

Responsorial Psalm (Ps 95): We should not be so bound up in earthly cares that we are unable to hear the voice of God speaking in our consciences.

Second Reading (Col 3:1-5, 9-11): Paul tells us that our lives should be Christ-centered and have Christ-values. If we have really died with Christ to the things the world esteems, why do we let worldly values still influence us?

Third Reading (Lk 12:13-21): Here Christ teaches us clearly and forcefully the foolishness of placing worth on earthly values. Wealth guarantees us nothing in eternal values. Those who rely on earthly goods will one day find them all reduced to ashes.

Thought for the Day: We live in a world of greed where men struggle to store up worldly goods, solely for the pleasure of possessions and the power they give. Yet, in God's sight all this is nothing. They can be lost in a moment. Then the only wealth we have is that which we have banked with God.

Nineteenth Sunday of the Year   < C

Theme: The true Christian lives a life of simple and uncompromising faith.

First Reading (Wis 18:6-9): The faith of the Israelites was confirmed in their deliverance from Egypt and in the punishment of their captors. This last book of the Old Testament praises that faith.

Responsorial Psalm (Ps 33): A hymn of thanks to God for His choice of us.

Second Reading (Heb 11:1-2, 8-9): St. Paul gives us a clear definition of faith: confident assurance in that which we hope for, and conviction about things we do not understand. He extols Abraham as a supreme example of complete faith.

Third Reading (Lk 12:32-48): Some writers see in this text a warning from Jesus to the leaders of Israel. He is making His final journey to Jerusalem, and this is their last chance to receive Him. There is a message here for all of us in the answer to Peter's question. The Son of Man is going to come to each one of us. Let us be ready.

Thought for the Day: Are we living a life of faith in God or one of trust in the values of the world? Does Christ hold the central position in my life from which I make my decisions and plans each day? This is the true test of our faith. Unless Christ is the center of all our actions, our faith is but lip service.

Twentieth Sunday of the Year   < C

Theme: God's prophets are without honor among their own people. Yet we must listen to them and sacrifice anything for the will of God.

First Reading (Jer 38:4-6, 8-10): Jeremiah's prophecies were similar to those of Jesus. He foretold the destruction of Judah by the Babylonian armies, the razing of the temple. Similarly to Christ, no one would listen to him. He was ignored and persecuted.

Responsorial Psalm (Ps 40): Jeremiah called on God to rescue him from the pit, and his prayer was answered.

Second Reading (Heb 12:1-4): Paul points to Jesus as an example for his converts. Like themselves, Jesus was persecuted for His beliefs. He endured and conquered. Therefore, Paul's converts have no reason to be despondent. They too can conquer in Christ.

Third Reading (Lk 12:49-53): Like last Sunday's Gospel, there are a number of meanings here. Christ's words refer to himself, His disciples, and those who will come after them. Jesus is on His way to His death; He would like to avoid what lies ahead, but it is something He must endure. His own fire must consume His followers. The fire He sets upon earth will divide even those who are close by blood. But no sacrifice is too great for the person who willingly serves the Master, whose fire will purify us and be a beacon to the world.

Thought for the Day: It is not popular to follow Christ, and any sacrifice must be made to do so, even the sacrifice of family and friends. People will laugh at the true Christian and call him or her foolish, but the fire of God's love will sustain faith.

Twenty-first Sunday of the Year   < C

Theme: Today's Scriptures have a messianic harmony: Christ's message is for all peoples of all times.

First Reading (Is 66:18-21): Isaiah is the messianic prophet of the Old Testament. He more than any other saw that the Messiah would draw people from east and west, non-Jews, to share His kingdom. The whole world will be joined in praise of God.

Responsorial Psalm (Ps 116): The Good News belongs to the whole world. Let every man and woman and child proclaim it to the nations!

Second Reading (Heb 12:5-7, 11-13): At first glance, the expression that whom the Lord loves He chastises seems contradictory, but when we compare this to life within the human family, we can see the wisdom. Those who loved God the most suffered the most, but none more than God's own Son, Jesus Christ. Can we not, therefore, find a reason in the suffering God permits to come our way?

Third Reading (Lk 13:22-30): Jesus continues His journey to Jerusalem, during which he makes the prophecy again that the Jews will be lost through their own doing and His kingdom will be opened to all nations, as even Isaiah foretold.

Thought for the Day: The Church belongs to all. If I keep my religion to myself, I am failing in the mission to which I was called in baptism.

Twenty-second Sunday of the Year   < C

Theme: Humility is the theme of the Mass today. Sirach extols this virtue, while Christ compares the proud and the humble.

First Reading (Sir 3:17-20, 28-29): We become great by being humble. Humility is a recognition of the truth. Its foundation is self-knowledge and a realization of our proper relationship with God.

Responsorial Psalm (Ps 68): A pre-vision of the Beatitudes. God makes a home for the poor, lonely, forsaken and imprisoned.

Second Reading (Heb 12:18-19, 22-24): Just preceding this reading, St. Paul tells his readers that they should seek that holiness without which one can never see the Lord. He now explains that this holiness is not in some distant and mysterious place, but in the Church, the new Jerusalem, where all will be made perfect and enabled to inherit heaven. This again is the humility of truth.

Third Reading (Lk 14:1, 7-14): Jesus returns to His attack on the religious establishment of His time by telling the parable wherein the lowly are exalted. In the second part of the Gospel He reminds us that our good deeds should not be to those who can repay us in kind, but to the poor and humble who have nothing to offer in return.

Thought for the Day: In His parable, Jesus was not merely rebuking the proud Pharisees but also instructing His disciples, among whom we are numbered. As Christians we must serve the poor and lowly, not only with alms, but by active efforts to transform our society, in which injustices exist. One way of doing this is through our votes, by voting only for those officials who have the good of our fellow citizens at heart, and not their own welfare.

Twenty-third Sunday of the Year   <   C

Theme: Of one's self, a person cannot understand or reach God, but by taking thought and using God's grace we can reach the brotherhood of which Paul speaks.

First Reading (Wis 9:13-18): Wisdom is a gift of the Holy Spirit which enables a person to judge rightly the things that pertain to everlasting life and to appreciate the divine over the earthly. Yet one cannot get wisdom by oneself without God's help.

Responsorial Psalm (Ps 90): The psalmist begs for wisdom, without which all is like changing grass.

Second Reading (Phlm 1:9-10, 12-17): This reading gives an unusual insight into Paul. Onesimus was a slave who ran away from his master in Greece. He was converted by Paul in Rome, and then served Paul, who was in prison. Paul sends him back to his owner, a Christian, asking that he be received as a brother and suggesting that he be allowed to return to help Paul in Rome. Paul is not trying to change the social structure of the Roman Empire, an impossible task. He does hope he can accomplish the same end by changing Philemon's heart to see not a slave but a fellow Christian.

Third Reading (Lk 14:25-33): There are two thoughts in today's Gospel. We must take up our own individual cross and follow the Master willingly. We must also carefully calculate what this will cost us. The costs may be great, but only by realizing them can we make the full commitment that Jesus expects of us.

Thought for the Day: In the readings today the Church is telling us how to live — wisely, with compassion for others, and with complete dedication to Christ. There are many ways to follow Christ; for some it is the active life of priest, brother or sister; for others it is work in behalf of the needy in the world; for all it is patient and steady faith.

Twenty-fourth Sunday of the Year   <   C

Theme: Forgiveness by the Father is the dominant note of today's liturgy. Because of the examples of the past, we can be confident of His forgiveness today.

First Reading (Ex 32:7-11, 13-14): The Jews were a hardheaded people, often forgetting their God. Even after their delivery from Egypt, they use Moses' absence to erect a golden idol. God would destroy them but is merciful because of the plea of Moses.

Responsorial Psalm (Ps 51): The psalmist begs God's forgiveness in confidence that his plea will be heard.

Second Reading (1 Tm 1:12-17): Paul recounts his own sins, reminding Timothy that God dealt mercifully with him. Our forgiveness in the New Covenant comes from the Father through Jesus.

Third Reading (Lk 15:1-32): Jesus proclaims that He has come to grant forgiveness to sinners, to save that which was lost. To illustrate His teaching, He tells His famous parable of the Prodigal Son and how he was welcomed back by his father. The implication is that no matter how far we stray, God is always ready to welcome us home.

Thought for the Day: Forgiveness is a key virtue for the Christian. In the Our Father we ask forgiveness for ourselves in the same measure as we forgive others. The Beatitude reminds us, "Blessed are the merciful." Every day we must be prepared to forgive — in our families, with friends, even those who would deliberately injure us. We also need forgiveness for ourselves, remembering always that it must be accompanied by a resolution to amend our lives and grow closer to God.

Twenty-fifth Sunday of the Year   <   C

Theme: The concern of the Christian is for all God's children, but he should have particular affection for the poor and needy.

First Reading (Am 8:4-7): Amos was a champion of God's justice. In today's reading the prophet thunders against social injustice. He defends the poor against rich oppressors, reminding the poor that God will never forget the crimes committed against them.

Responsorial Psalm (Ps 113): God's justice will avenge the poor by raising them to equality with all in His judgment.

Second Reading (1 Tm 2:1-8): Paul tells the Christian community to pray for all. He specifically singles out prayer for those in authority, even though in many cases that authority is persecuting the Church. Respect for authority is fundamental to Christian belief because authority comes from God and shares in His supreme authority. Even Christ submitted to authority at the cost of His life.

Third Reading (Lk 16:1-13): The message of the Gospel echoes the words of Amos. In this devious parable Christ is warning the Jewish leaders that they should read the signs of the times, namely that the kingdom of God is at hand. They had better use their position to gain God's favor. They had better rid themselves of what they have extorted from the poor. They must choose money or God, for they cannot have both.

Thought for the Day: Every pope since Leo XIII has stressed the need of social justice in the world. In days when it was unpopular, and long before the communists arrived, the Church was preaching the message of today's liturgy. Vatican Council II spoke out strongly about a more equal distribution of the wealth God has given the world. The veiled warning to the Jewish religious leaders applies to the economically powerful of our own times. Every Christian must be committed to social justice; any other attitude is a scandal.

Twenty-sixth Sunday of the Year   < C

Theme: The liturgy this Sunday carries forward the theme of last Sunday. The complacent rich will be punished, and the suffering poor shall be rewarded. Again a beatitude is echoed: Blessed are the poor in spirit for they shall see God.

First Reading (Am 6:1, 4-7): The social prophet Amos continues his denunciation of the rich. The Assyrian armies are moving on the northern kingdom, and the rich will be the first to suffer God's retribution when they come. Their punishment will be for the neglect of the poor.

Responsorial Psalm (Ps 146): A hymn of praise to God for His protection of the hungry and oppressed.

Second Reading (1 Tm 6:11-16): Although Paul's summary exhortation is addressed to Timothy as bishop and priest and through him to all priests, each one of us must live according to God's laws. In the spirit of today's liturgy, we should be particularly concerned with our relationship to all people.

Third Reading (Lk 16:19-31): It is difficult for anyone to miss the point of this parable. All the riches of the world will do a man no good after death. In God's justice all will be leveled and those who have suffered on earth will be amply rewarded. The parable is also a warning to the Jewish leaders who are refusing to listen to Him, while simple men, such as fishermen, follow Him with devotion.

Thought for the Day: We cannot, like Cain, ask the rhetorical question "Am I my brother's keeper?" The fact is that we are. We may object to the social and economic discrimination in our own country, but what about the vast gulf that separates Americans and people of the Third World? What are my obligations towards a Tanzanian or a Peruvian Indian? How do I apply the Gospel to them?

Twenty-seventh Sunday of the Year   <   C

Theme: Faith is the keynote of today's liturgy. It is absolutely necessary for salvation.

First Reading (Heb 1:2-3, 2:2-4): Habakkuk is asking God a question that many have asked: Why should sinners and unbelievers prosper and be able to inflict pain and suffering on God's own people? God's reply is that He is testing those whom He loves and that justice will be done. God then says something that has had a strong influence on Christian theology: The just man, because of his faith, will find redemption.

Responsorial Psalm (Ps 95): God is always speaking to us,

and the person of faith does not close his or her heart to Him.
Second Reading (2 Tm 1:6-8, 13-14): Paul is writing his last letter and knows that death is approaching. The most important message he can give his disciple Timothy is that he should strengthen his faith.
Third Reading (Lk 17:5-10): The apostles ask Our Lord to increase their faith. Our Lord replies that a man is not rewarded for doing what he is expected to do. Yet it is in the careful performance of our daily activities that our faith will grow.
Thought for the Day: Many people confuse faith and knowledge. They think that because they have a knowledge of Catholic doctrine that they have the faith. Faith does not need knowledge. It is a complete trust in God and His Word. All of us are tested in life when we suffer some reversal or loss. It is then when we know how deep our faith really is.

Twenty-eighth Sunday of the Year < C

Theme: God's grace belongs to all and it alone can save us from spiritual death.
First Reading (2 Kgs 5:14-17): It is significant that Elisha the prophet should cure a foreigner and nonbeliever, even though the latter thought that Elisha's conditions were foolish. The incident ends with the pagan pledging to serve the true God.
Responsorial Psalm (Ps 98): A hymn of praise because "the Lord has shown his salvation to the nations."
Second Reading (2 Tm 2:8-13): Paul reminds Timothy that Jesus was raised from the dead and that nothing is impossible for God. If we lead a Christian life, we too will rise and reign with Him.
Third Reading (Lk 17:11-19): Again God's power is shown in the curing of the ten lepers, but it is only a hated foreigner who returns to give praise. Luke is reminding us of Christ's ability to forgive sin, a gift of salvation that will be offered to all men.
Thought for the Day: Not everyone who cries "Lord, Lord!" will be saved but he who does the will of God. Jesus offers hope to every man on earth, and this is a message we should share with all, particularly those who know Him not.

Twenty-ninth Sunday of the Year   <   C

Theme: The dominant note of the liturgy today is one of constant and persevering prayer in the confident belief that God will always hear us.

First Reading (Ex 17:8-13): Although Moses was specially loved by God and appointed by Him to deliver the Israelites to freedom, in this passage we learn that even Moses must persevere in prayer, despite personal fatigue. There is a clear lesson for all of us.

Responsorial Psalm (Ps 121): God will guard us from all evil. We can place our confidence in Him.

Second Reading (2 Tm 3:14; 4:2): Paul is writing his final instructions to his friend and disciple, Timothy, exhorting him to be faithful to his duties of bishop and priest. In today's reading he reminds Timothy of the importance of Sacred Scriptures as a source of wisdom and faith. This lesson applies to all of us.

Third Reading (Lk 18:1-8): Perseverance in prayer is a repeated message Christ gives to His apostles as He makes His way to Jerusalem and His death. He tells the parable of this reading in order to teach that God will respond lovingly to prayer.

Thought for the Day: Many people begin projects, but far fewer ever finish them. The world is full of half-finished things. For the Christian, perseverance is a necessary virtue. Christ gives us His personal example as He determinedly makes His way to His death. Besides His example we have His teaching: "Pray always."

Thirtieth Sunday of the Year   <   C

Theme: The prayer of the humble is particularly pleasing to God.

First Reading (Sir 35:12-14, 16-18): God listens to the prayer of the humble. Sirach places Old Testament emphasis on the widow and orphan, symbol for the world's oppressed. Again there is a warning to the rich and powerful, who because of their status do not feel that they need God.

Responsorial Psalm (Ps 34): God responds to the prayer of the poor and needy.

Second Reading (2 Tm 4:6-8, 16-18): There is a great sadness in this closing part of Paul's letter to his beloved disciple, Timothy. Death is close at hand, and Paul is abandoned by all, but his confidence in God never wavers. He compares his life to a race which is now about over, and at the end of which he will receive his heavenly prize.

Third Reading (Lk 18:9-14): God is not awed by a person's rank or privilege. Nor is He impressed by good works that lack humble faith. Christ uses the Pharisee as an example of hypocrisy while the publican, who was cut off from Jewish life, receives forgiveness because of his humility.

Thought for the Day: St. Paul is an example of a man truly humble. He used the talents God gave him to advance the kingdom. Martyrdom is to be his reward, not a long life of ease, riches and pleasure. The liturgy today challenges our values. A cruel death is not something esteemed by the world. Although Paul has served Christ fully and faithfully, he expects no material gains but eagerly looks forward to his heavenly reward.

Thirty-first Sunday of the Year   <   C

Theme: God loves His creation and stays His justified wrath even though He is offended. The proof of His love was the sending of His Son, who came to save those who are lost.

First Reading (Wis 11:22 — 12:2): This is the strongest expression in the Old Testament of God's love for all creation and the reason for it. God spares us because He loves us and is patient with us that we might repent and return His love.

Responsorial Psalm (Ps 145): A hymn of praise for God's love for His creation.

Second Reading (2 Thes 1:11 — 2:2): Because of the persecutions and trouble which have befallen the Church in Thessalonia, many converts have come to believe that the Second Coming is close at hand. Paul tells them that he has never preached this because no one knows when Christ will come again. But we must always be ready. He indicates later in this passage that there is much yet to be done.

Third Reading (Lk 19:1-10): This delightful story of little Zacchaeus illustrates clearly the message of today's liturgy.

Christ did not come to save the saved but, as Luke tells us, to save that which was lost.

Thought for the Day: To meet Jesus is to have one's values changed. Our God is a God of love who seeks the salvation of all. To accomplish this, He sent His only Son to us. Today we meet Jesus through the liturgy and New Testament. Do we seek these encounters? What do they mean to us?

Thirty-second Sunday of the Year   <   C

Theme: As we approach the end of the liturgical year, the attention of the Church turns to the last things: our resurrection and the Second Coming of Christ. Today the Church places emphasis on our resurrection.

First Reading (2 Mc 7:1-2, 9-14): The Jewish theology of personal resurrection developed slowly, but in the book of Maccabees it is clearly understood. Today's story of the martyrdom of a mother and her seven sons, who preferred death to apostasy, occurred during one of the violent persecutions of the Jews that took place not long before the birth of Christ. They die in the firm belief that they will rise from the dead.

Responsorial Psalm (Ps 17): After death the just man will eternally be in God's presence.

Second Reading (2 Thes 2:16 — 3:5): Immediately preceding today's reading, Paul has been answering questions of the Thessalonians about the Second Coming. In the verse immediately before this reading he exhorts the Thessalonians to "stand firm. Hold fast to the traditions you received from us. . ." In today's reading he exhorts them to continue in the faith which has been bestowed upon them.

Third Reading (Lk 20:27-38): Jesus now begins the last ministry of His mission, that to Jerusalem itself. He engages in discussion with the narrow and rigorous Sadducees, who held only the five books of Moses and denied the resurrection. Jesus goes directly to the heart of their beliefs, referring to the absurdity of their teaching that an heir should not die without sons. He tells them that no one dies in the eyes of God.

Thought for the Day: Our Christian beliefs demand our assent to the Second Coming of Christ, but we do not know when this will happen. We do know know that for each of us, individual judgment is close at hand. Each of us can prepare for the day of our judgment and eternal life with God.

Thirty-third Sunday of the Year   < C

Theme: The Church now turns our attention to the end of the world, which will coincide with the Second Coming of Christ. Our Lord tells the signs that will be present, but since we do not know when this will be, we must always be ready.

First Reading (Mal 3:19-20): This reading of the prophet Malachi is selected to correspond to the message of the Gospel. Malachi is responding to a question that has plagued man from the beginning: How do we explain evil and wrong in the world? Malachi tells us that God renders justice and that there will be a day of reckoning for evildoers.

Responsorial Psalm (Ps 98): Echoes the theme of Malachi. The Lord will come with the rule of justice.

Second Reading (2 Thes 3:7-12): Although Paul has instructed his followers to await the Second Coming, they are not to do so in idleness. They should follow his example and keep busy in their daily tasks. He reminds them that even he works to support himself.

Third Reading (Lk 21:5-19): Luke, following the plan of his narrative, has his attention fixed on the destruction of Jerusalem. But this will not be the end of the world. Even in the final trials, the true Christian will remain secure in his confidence in Christ. This confidence will enable him to endure any trials which may come his way.

Thought for the Day: Although we must look to the future, we must not forget the fact that we must live in the present. What we do today is our part in salvation history.

Feast of Christ the King   < C

Theme: The Church chooses the last Sunday of the liturgical year to commemorate the Feast of Christ the King. The readings remind us that Christ is king of this world and the next, but it is a kingship that many will misunderstand.

First Reading (2 Sm 5:1-3): The Israelites looked beyond David to his line of descendants, from whom their Messiah would come. In this short reading David is proclaimed King of Israel, and it was to his descendants that Christ belonged.

Responsorial Psalm (Ps 122): A hymn sung by pilgrims on their way to the temple in Jerusalem.

Second Reading (Col 1:12-20): Paul's testimony to Christ, who has dominion over all, expresses the fundamental of his teaching that it is in Christ that everything has its being.

Third Reading (Lk 23:35-43): This Gospel presents us with the enigma of Christianity — a king whose throne is a cross. The Jews proclaimed Jesus a king in mockery and gave Him a court of thieves. Yet in His last moments, He gives what no other king can give — forgiveness of sins.

Thought for the Day: Today's liturgy ends Luke's account of the long journey of Jesus to Jerusalem. It ends not in visible triumph but in death. Yet in that death He earned His right to kingship and the government of all. While His kingdom is partly in this world, His kingship is of another. While all of us must work to extend His kingdom here on earth, our reward will come in His kingdom of heaven.

Holy Days

Assumption of Mary (Aug. 15)

Theme: Mary's whole life proclaims the greatness of God. What God accomplished in Mary, He will accomplish in each of us through the Resurrection.

First Reading (Rv 11:19, 12:1-6, 10): This section begins the heart of the Book of Revelation. Evil, presented by the monster, seeks to destroy the celestial woman and her son. Protected by God, she gives birth safely. Her child will destroy the monster and bring happiness to the world.

Responsorial Psalm (Ps 45): A royal psalm composed for the wedding of an Israelite king and a foreign princess. It is applied here to Mary.

Second Reading (1 Cor 15:20-26): The parallelism and contrast between Adam and Christ is a common Pauline teaching, just as religious literature compares Eve with Mary. Through Christ our own resurrection is ensured, and Mary, because she is the mother of Jesus, has a role in this.

Third Reading (Lk 1:38-56): After the Annunciation, Mary hastens to her cousin, Elizabeth, to be with her as she carries John the Baptist. In response to Elizabeth's greeting, Mary utters the celebrated Magnificat.

Thought for the Day: The Magnificat gives us the best insight into Mary of any scriptural passage. It shows her to be an intelligent woman with great mastery of the Old Testament. It shows her to be a woman of thoughtful conviction and firm faith. There are deep theological insights in the passage — insights into the salvation and liberation that will be brought by Christ.

Feast of All Saints (Nov. 1)

Theme: We honor all those who remained loyal to Christ and His Father and who are now enjoying the vision and intimacy of God's presence.

First Reading (Rv 7:2-4, 9-14): John's vision of heaven is one of a place with people of every nation, race, tribe and language in a number beyond counting. It shows the universality of redemption.

Responsorial Psalm (Ps 23): Salvation is for the pure of heart, those not attached to the worthless values of the world.·

Second Reading (1 Jn 3:1-3): We understand God now only through the eyes of faith. The vision of God to come will be intimate and immediate. The Christian who possesses this vision will be like Christ, whose relation to God the Father is unique.

Third Reading (Mt 5:1-12): The Beatitudes proclaimed a moral revolution in which even the least could partake. They were opposed to all the conventional values of the Greek and Roman worlds. They do, however, require an active participation on the part of the Christian.

Thought for the Day: The Church has two purposes: to give honor to God and to provide salvation for its members. Therefore, those who are saved are a cause for great rejoicing. Outside of a few canonized saints, their names are unknown to us. On this day, however, the Church calls on its members here on earth to rejoice with those who have gone before us in salvation.

Immaculate Conception (Dec. 8)

Theme: We celebrate the Virgin Mary's conception, kept free through the power of God from all stain of original sin.

First Reading (Gn 3:9-15): The account of the fall of Adam and Eve. Evil comes into the world, and mankind will be subject to it. Adam blames Eve for his sin, and indirectly also accuses God of responsibility.

Responsorial Psalm (Ps 98): God alone gives salvation.

Second Reading (Eph 1:3-6, 11-12): Paul omits his usual introduction to begin his epistle with praise of God for revealing His plan of salvation in Jesus Christ. What was lost through the sin of Adam and Eve has been regained by the sacrifice of Christ.

Third Reading (Lk 1:26-38): This is the familiar story of the Annunciation. By her consent to Gabriel's request, Mary becomes the new Eve. What the first Eve lost through sin, Mary now regains by her obedience to God's will. Living the will of God was Mary's quest in life.

Thought for the Day: It is a dogma of the Church to which all Catholics must give assent that Mary from the moment of her conception was kept free of all stain of original sin. As Pope Pius IX declared, Catholic tradition has held Mary "not only immaculate, but entirely immaculate; not only innocent, but most innocent; not only spotless, but most spotless . . . God alone excepted, she is superior to all."

Supplanting Feasts

Presentation of Our Lord (Feb. 2)

Theme: Although in the new liturgy the Church does not often replace the liturgy of the ordinary Sunday, today's feast is an exception. It is the public introduction of our Lord to the world. While it is a day of joy, there is also a caution because Christ's teaching will refine and purify. While it will be salvation for many, it will also be a reason for the condemnation of others.

First Reading (Mal 3:1-4): The prophet Malachi sees Christ as God's expected messenger, but he also warns of the retribution He will bring.

Responsorial Psalm (Ps 24): This is the great prophetic hymn of praise to Jesus, the king of glory.

Second Reading (Heb 2:14-18): Paul extols the humanity of Christ, assuring his readers that because Christ was also a man like themselves, He understands human nature. It is this understanding that enables Him to help men to be freed of the slavery of sins and to withstand temptation.

Third Reading (Lk 2:22-40): Luke dwells at length upon the traditional presentation of the firstborn to the Lord. His purpose is not only to show that Christ made himself subject to the law of Moses, but to recount the prophecies of Simeon and Anna. Simeon's prophecy that the Child will be the cause for the rise and downfall of many in Israel applies to each one of us. Simeon and Anna represent the long-waiting Israel, but unlike most of Israel they recognized the greatness of the Divine Child.

Thought for the Day: Each of us should take to heart the warning that underlies today's liturgy. Christ is our salvation, but if we ignore His laws and His way of life we are writing our own judgment — a condemnation that is frightening because it can be for all eternity. Will our Christianity be the cause of our salvation or our loss? Each must answer this question.

Birth of John the Baptist (June 24)

Theme: "No greater man was ever born of woman," was the accolade Jesus bestowed on his cousin John. He was the one chosen by God to prepare the way for Jesus.

First Reading (Is 49:1-6): Isaiah sings of the Servant of Yahweh, whom the Church likens to John the Baptist, a sharp-edged sword, a polished arrow. Called by God, although his life seems to have ended in failure, he has not "toiled in vain."

Responsorial Psalm (Ps 139): No one knows us like God, for it is He who made us.

Second Reading (Acts 13:22-26): Paul tells us Christ's coming was announced by John. Luke (the author) regards John as belonging to the Old Law. Luke stresses John's subordinate role, perhaps as a polemic to a cult John's followers had formed after his death.

Third Reading (Lk 1:57-66): This is the account of the birth and naming of John. The miraculous is here, and there is no reason to doubt the wonderment of the neighborhood: "What is this child to be?"

Thought for the Day: Although John possessed great charisms in his own right, his true greatness was his cooperation with God's plan. Filled with the Holy Spirit from birth, he is expressly called to be a prophet. Some make John the last prophet of the Old Testament, while others see him as a bridge between the Old and the New Law. He is the new Elijah, heralding the messianic era.

Sts. Peter and Paul (June 29)

Theme: The blood of martyrs is the seed of Christianity. Sts. Peter and Paul planted the Church with their blood.

First Reading (Acts 12:1-11): Peter came from Bethsaida, a town on Lake Galilee, later moving to Capernaum. He was the brother of Andrew, also an apostle. After Pentecost, Peter's primacy in the Church was never challenged. He worked miracles, and God in turn worked miracles for him, as in today's reading. After serving the Church in Jerusalem and Antioch, he went to Rome; hence the successor to his See is regarded as head of the Church.

Responsorial Psalm (Ps 34): A Davidic psalm which here refers to the deliverance of Peter from Herod.

Second Reading (2 Tm 4:6-8, 17-18): Paul, called directly by Christ, has always been considered an apostle. From a persecutor of Christianity, he became the great Apostle to the Gentiles. After perilous missionary journeys, he was finally taken a prisoner to Rome. It was Paul who made Christianity a worldwide religion and profoundly influenced the religious thinking of mankind. Before his execution by Nero (c. 64-65), he wrote Timothy this statement of his beliefs.

Third Reading (Mt 16:13-19): This is one of the most important readings of the New Testament. Christ clearly states the establishment of His Church, giving the governing power to Peter, and through him to his successors. The power of the keys gives all authority to that Church.

Thought for the Day: Peter and Paul are models for our faith, a faith based on service to our fellowman.

Triumph of the Cross (Sept. 14)

Theme: The Church pauses a moment in the usual Sunday liturgies to direct our attention to what the Cross of Jesus gained for us. His death gave promise of our own resurrection.

First Reading (Nm 21:4-9): Although God in many and various ways showed His particular love for the people of Israel, they often forgot His kindnesses and remembered their own trials and thus grumbled against Him. To remind them of His power, God sometimes had to punish them. This incident in the Jews' long journey to the Promised Land shows both God's punishment and concern.

Responsorial Psalm (Ps 78): Despite the stubbornness of the Jews and the fact that they often departed from God's ways,

He showed them many favors, turning back His anger with mercy.

Second Reading (Phil 2:6-11): Christ gave the supreme example of obedience by delivering himself up to death on the cross. For Paul, this is *the* proof that Jesus Christ is Lord.

Third Reading (Jn 3:13-17): "God so loved the world that He gave His only Son." Jesus himself offers this proof of God's love. He further testifies that belief in Him promises eternal life. But belief means nothing unless our actions follow from it.

Thought for the Day: Last week the liturgy was concerned with the problem of suffering, and today's liturgy furthers that theme. Jesus could not do anything evil, and in submitting himself to suffering and death, He was showing us that suffering is not evil in itself. Sometimes it is undergone for the good of others, and always it is the most direct route to God. The Cross of Christ is the answer to the world's flight from pain and suffering. It represents not the world's but God's values.

Dedication of Lateran Basilica (Nov. 9)

Theme: The house of God is an especially sacred place, and the Church has a special feast to commemorate its major houses of worship. The holy character of the building comes not from brick and mortar, but from the faith of the people worshiping there.

First Reading (2 Chr 5:6-10, 13; 6:2): Jewish life centered about the Temple because it signified God's presence among the Israelites. Much of Old Testament history is concerned with the building, destruction and rebuilding of the Temple. Even today the ruins of the Temple are a place of worship for both Jews and Christians.

Responsorial Psalm (Ps 84): This great psalm of David extols the house of God and David's desire to spend his days in worship there.

Second Reading (1 Cor 3:9-13, 16-17): "Are you not aware that you are the temple of God, and that the Spirit of God dwells in you?" Paul asks his converts in Corinth. Conscious of his Jewish background and the holiness of the Temple in Jerusalem, Paul is also aware of the exaggerations and legalisms which had grown up around the Temple in Jerusalem. Just as Christ had compared himself to the Temple, Paul tells his converts that their bodies too are sacred. The Holy Spirit dwells in them in a special way, since baptism and the Eucharist give them spiritual life.

Third Reading (Lk 19:1-10): Faith is the cornerstone on which the Church is built. Zacchaeus was looked down upon by Jews because he collected taxes for the Romans. Christ went past the externals and saw a man of faith and charity. He told Zacchaeus, "Today salvation has come to this house."

Thought for the Day: When most people think of Rome, they think of St. Peter's Basilica, but the Basilica of St. John Lateran is the oldest and first in rank of all Christian basilicas. It is the episcopal seat of the Bishop of Rome, the pope. The grounds and original basilica were donated by Constantine as headquarters for the pope. While we commemorate the dedication of this ancient church, the liturgy really focuses attention on Christian living, telling us that our salvation comes not through externals, but through our beliefs and actions.